RED IN THE CENTRE

Through a Crooked Lens

MONTE DWYER

Monyer Pty Ltd

RED IN THE CENTRE
Through a Crooked Lens

Published by
Monyer Pty Ltd

Ph 0412 422 699

Email info@monte.com.au

ISBN: 978-0-646-52740-6

Printed in Australia by Griffin Press

10 9 8 7 6 5 4 3 2 1

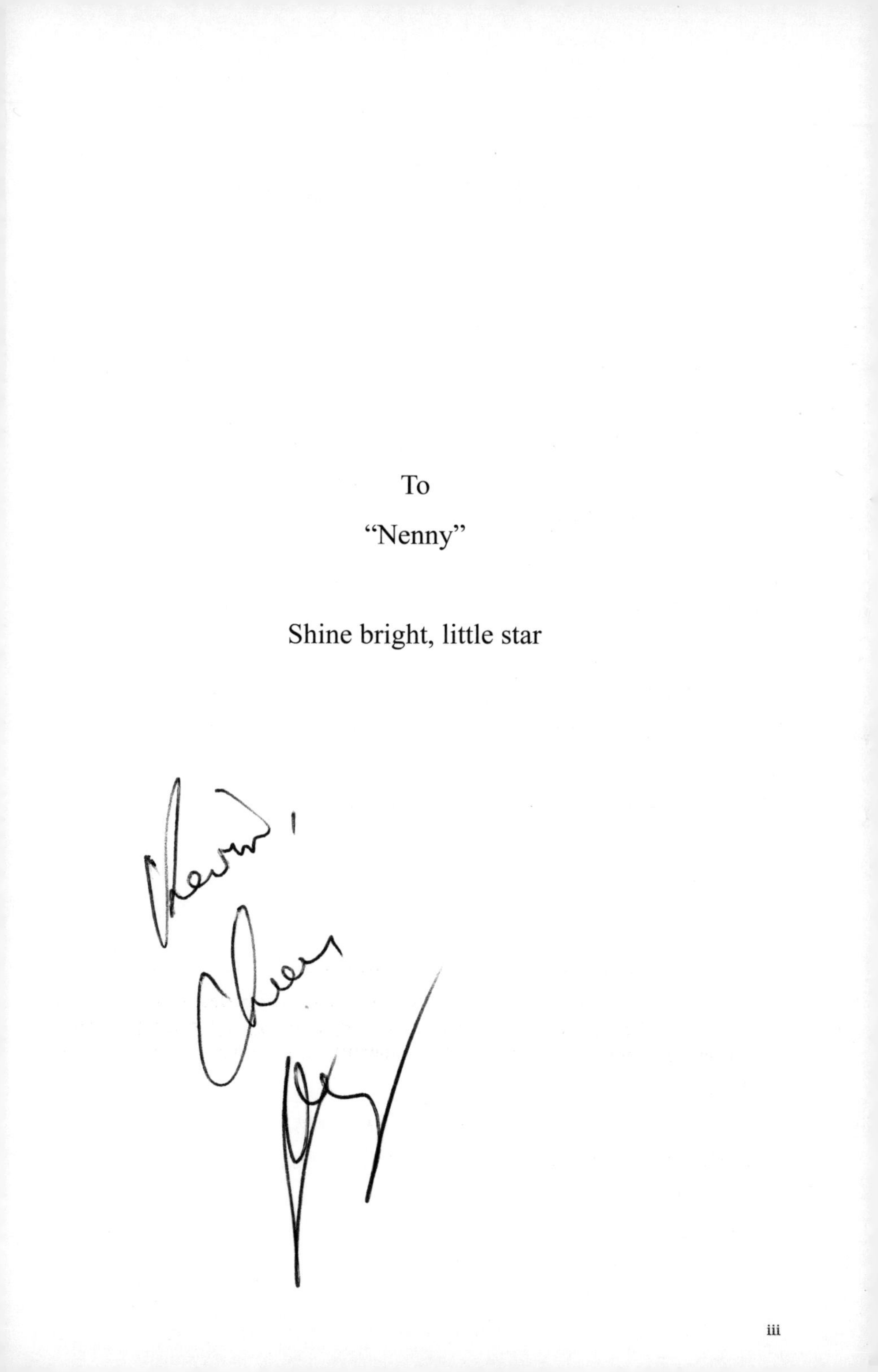

To

"Nenny"

Shine bright, little star

ALSO BY MONTE

BOOKS:

Slapped by an Angel

Red in the Centre – *The Australian Bush Through Urban Eyes*

PLAYS:

I Would've Written

Tadpoles

Son

VIDEOS:

Monte Dwyer's Flying Cirrus – *How I Learned to Stop Worrying and Love the Weather*

Red in the Centre – *Through a Crooked Lens*

MUSIC:

Self Titled EP

Red in the Centre EP

Red in the Centre CD

All product available at **www.monte.com.au** while stocks last.
Books also distributed by Dennis Jones and Associates.

THANKS

To Adam Boland of Sunrise for having the courage to try something new; Winnebago for "giving me another car to trash"; Australia Network and Tourism Australia for sponsoring the second half of the trip; my draft readers Terry Dwyer, Ross Gallen, Adrielle Drury, Iain Riggs & James Mansfield for their intelligent feedback; Emma Sutton of Digital Art for the cover design and text layout; the many mechanics, auto-electricians and 'roadside assistants' around the country who helped me keep Claude the Obstinate going; ditto Tom at Old Mac Toyota for keeping the parts coming from Japan; my contributors who spoke with candour and generosity about their lives and gave heart to this book; and a special thanks to the Wood family for providing me sanctuary to shape this work at a time of great personal hardship in their own lives.

Cheers

Monte

FOREWORD

I'm thrilled to be asked to write the Foreword for *Through a Crooked Lens,* as it's the icing on the Monte Dwyer cake that all Northern Territory people have enjoyed for so many years. Just as John Clark and Brian Dawe wind up the 7.30 Report on a whimsical note each week, Northern Territorians used to delight in the fact that, at the end of the ABC News, Monte Dwyer would present the Weather Report like nobody else had ever done before. Then he went on to National Commercial TV and slayed them. It was a laugh a minute, yet, importantly, we got the weather information we needed. Now Monte has taken to touring the outback and writing delightful books like this, to allow us to share his very different experiences. It is a great art to be able to tell a story that sends yourself up. Monte does it naturally: I guess he would say it's an acquired skill as he has had lots of practice.

People who don't have tickets on themselves, or take themselves too seriously, are often good listeners – one of life's greatest attributes. Monte has it in spades. He is able to uncover the true worth of the authentic characters, to send up those full of pomp and their own importance, to take us into the unknown regions that even the most experienced travellers among us seem to have missed. For he is always looking to do things and go to places that might not even rate consideration by Bill Bryson.

This is a delightful follow-up to the 2008 book and CD, RED IN THE CENTRE, a fine production that took us with Monte on a Round Australia blitz. His songs and his prose are fresh and sharp. He views life with a Jack Nicholson like, quizzical overview, a

Why is this thus?disdain.

Monte reminds me of so many people. He reminds me of Bob Dylan when he quotes Dylan; "Takes courage to sing with a voice like mine". OK, he's not Caruso. But he has things to say that are important, and you find yourself reading the lyric sheet closely and admiring the Dylanesque wordsmithing. He reminds me of Pat Drummond, who over a lot of years has built up an immense following, a clientele who dwell on Pat's every incisive word. I think that slowly, surely, Monte Dwyer will establish a cult via books and albums like this. Australia needs it, if we are to remain a unique country where:

It's red in the Centre and blue all around
With a ribbon of gold in between
It's bigger than Texas and flatter than Spain
It's the best country I've ever seen

Get out there and sell it, Mont. Busk on the streets. Bail them up in the pubs. Nobody will do it better than you.

Ted Egan AO
Alice Springs
December 2009

CONTENTS

PREFACE

In 2007-8 I travelled Australia in a campervan sourcing and broadcasting stories for a national radio program. My brief was to supply three stories a week, so I talked to all comers from all walks, indeed anyone who'd pause long enough for me to grab the microphone, and documented the experience in a book called RED IN THE CENTRE, *The Australian Bush Through Urban Eyes,* and an accompanying CD of original music. When I launched RED IN THE CENTRE on the Seven Network's breakfast program, Sunrise, I grandly suggested to the show's Executive Producer that I could make television in the same 'shoot-from-the-hip' manner as I'd done for radio. He took me at my word and promptly armed me with a camera, a laptop loaded with professional editing software, and a Winnebago, and shuffled me straight back out there. Apart from knowing how to drive I was completely ill prepared.

Essentially *Through a Crooked Lens* is the second phase in the evolution of the RED IN THE CENTRE concept. From my early frustrations as I 'went to school' on the Sunrise experience, to my stumbling development as a freelance storyteller travelling the land in my own unreliable bus called Claude in search of material to commit to video, print or song, *Through a Crooked Lens* follows the journey right around the country to the very tip of mainland Australia. The companion DVD is a videologue of the second part of the trip (ie with Claude) and includes many of the stories contained herein.

It is my belief that in our mad rush to urbanise this country we are fast losing touch with an integral part of our national identity, ie the bush. As our city-centric media becomes flashier and more profit-driven, the extraordinary stories of ordinary Australians choosing to live their lives outside the narrow perimeters set by the mainstream are vanishing unrecorded. With RED IN THE CENTRE it is my objective to tell as many of these stories in as many possible ways as I am able.

Enjoy.
Monte

JE NE SAIS QUOI

Three months into the four-month agreement the good ship SS Sunrise cast me adrift without notice. Indeed I was effectively sacked while I was on air, which could've made for some interesting television if only I'd known it was happening.

The reason I didn't know, quite apart from being uninformed, was because I was doing a live cross from Peel Street, Tamworth, and the loud buzzing of six hundred guitars playing Smoke on the Water drowned out what the studio hosts were saying.

"They were saying goodbye," a mate rang to tell me after the show.

"But I haven't finished the agreed term."

"I think you'll find you have, mate."

He was right. There'd been a change of personnel back at Sunrise and the stand-in Executive Producer confirmed it. They'd pulled the pin on the Postcards series. The hosts had farewelled me on air. And not for the first time in television history had a verbal contract proved worthless.

You hear about this sort of treatment being dished out by the networks, but only to *other people*. Not important, indispensable people like *you*; creative linchpins capable of adding that little bit of *je ne sais quoi* every straight show needs to save it from mediocrity. But obviously the brains trust at Sunrise had decided they were right for *je ne sais quoi* at the moment, thanks, and I was free to peddle mine wherever the hell I wanted.

Under normal circumstances, of course, *je ne sais quoi* isn't the easiest thing in this country to peddle. To begin with nobody knows what it is. Most Anglo-Francais dictionaries translate it as "I know not what", or "an indefinable something," which makes it a hard sell right off the bat. Secondly, Australians are very wary of foreign-sounding products and most wouldn't be caught dead saying such a thing, let alone trying to spell it*.

Luckily I happened to be in Tamworth for Country Music Week, hand-selling books on the street, and I was in a perfect position to be flogging off some recently liberated *je ne sais quoi.* Country music crowds just love a bit of the old "I don't know what the hell it is but I like it anyway", because that's what the whole country music scene is all about. (I know, because I play the stuff and I haven't a clue what it is, either.)

Later in the day I got a call from the original Executive Producer of Sunrise – who'd since moved on to another show – apologising for the handling of the whole affair. And while he couldn't exactly promise me another series of Postcards once the dust settled, to his credit he did honour the original agreement.

"Do you want me to continue to file stories?" I asked him.

"No, just float around out there till we work out what to do with you."

"And keep sending you invoices?"

"Of course."

And with those two words all was forgiven. So for the next few weeks I drove Mother Theresa around shooting but not filing

* I always ring my sister, who owns one of those conversion dictionaries.

stories, obliging fans by posing for photos and generally behaving as though I was still a happy member of the Sunrise family. Even the staunchest fans saw nothing wrong with me driving the Winnebago around despite having seen me farewelled.

Interestingly when I left the Today Show all those years ago I did so of my own volition and everyone assumed I'd been sacked. This time I *had* been bumped and people assumed I was still employed, that I was just taking a break and would resume normal transmission as soon as the fault was rectified. I hoped they were right.

At one stage, camped in a caravan park in Lismore famous for hosting a murder a few years ago, I remember a couple of young boys of about twelve or thirteen riding up on their bicycles to say g'day.

"Aren't you that Monte guy off Sunrise?" one said.

"That's me."

"Cool," said the other.

"Why is that cool?"

"Because you can put us on telly and we'll be famous."

"I don't think so."

"Aww, why not?"

"Because you haven't got any *je ne sais quoi.*"

"Where can we get some?"

"Ask your father."

During the post-dismissal conversation with the stand-in EP he'd suggested a *poste mortem*, said he was interested in hearing any grievances I might have, so when I served my time and came in from the cold I sent an email to notify them of my safe arrival, and waited for a response.

After six weeks without one I sent another. This one was headed "Common Courtesy" and was far from pretty, but at least this time the response was immediate.

"Hey, Monte, maaaate, where are you?" It was the stand-in EP.

"Sydney. Got back the year before last."

"Great. Let's do lunch."

There is nothing, repeat *nothing* more important in television than lunch. If you get invited to lunch it means you're still in the game, you're still *somebody*. It means the big guy is prepared to take time out of his busy day to listen to a wretch like you shimmy for a toehold in his great world. Okay, so it was only yum cha at the local Chinese, but these are tough times and it was still lunch. I started feeling my old *je ne sais quoi* returning.

On the morning of the day of reckoning I got a call from his secretary. Lunch was off because he had an upset tummy and couldn't eat. Would I mind meeting at the office?

Well, at least the dog didn't eat his homework. I went in expecting very little and wasn't disappointed. There was to be no second series of Postcards and they weren't interested in any further input from me. Shame: I thought I was just getting the hang of things. I guess it must have been my *je ne sais quoi*.

HELP

In hindsight I should have known I was in trouble right from the start, when they handed me my camera kit in a recycle carry bag. That was my camera case: a red shopping bag. In it I had a digital video camera I'd never used before, microphones the like of which I'd never seen before and a tangle of cables like a bowl of cold spaghetti.

Then there was the software I didn't know how to use to edit the stories I didn't know how to shoot. It was all very well to design this stuff for the IT-challenged, but what about those of us even less credentialed than that? Technology hates me, always has. And it's a mutual thing, of course, but I'm the only one who cares.

To be fair they did give me some training, and just before I left I had two lessons. I listened hard, watched closely and remembered nothing. First time I sat down to edit a story I barely got beyond opening the program. I tried to ring my support guy at Apple but he'd gone to America. It was hard not to take it personally.

I also tried to reach my contacts back at the office but they weren't returning my calls. I'm not normally paranoid but the voices were louder than usual right about then.

Meanwhile I was sitting in a campervan in a caravan park in Bourke, western New South Wales, staring at my laptop screen and watching the lights flicker on some piece of equipment the technician had called a gateway. I didn't have a clue what function it served, but when he installed it he took the door off the cupboard "to let it breathe," he said. That sounded very much like it was alive, to me. It was alive and it hated me.

The temptation to blame someone else for my predicament was almost irresistible, but way down deep I knew it was all my doing. When I told the Executive Producer of Sunrise I could make television out of Red in the Centre I wasn't really thinking of the production realities. I meant the concept, the notion of "one man, one camera, one hell of a country" sort of thing. It sounded pretty cool to me at the time. And it obviously sounded cool enough for him to agree. Yet there I was, one day out and a long, long way from cool.

And not only was my head being worked over from the inside but every time I stood up I banged into something – the overhead cupboards which were anything but, the low-slung bed in the Luton peak (that's what *they* called it, don't ask me why), the exit door. They'd equipped me with a Winnebago for the trip and it was going to take some getting used to. I even started wearing my hat inside to soften the blows.

"I can't believe they've given you another vehicle to trash," was the unkind refrain from one of my mates when I told him I had a new campervan. I didn't have a great track record with these things, but the Winnebago was way ahead on points so far.

And still I was no closer to extracting my story from the editing program in any coherent form than I was when I first sat down. At least *then* I still knew where I was in the process. As it was I felt like a drunk retracing his steps trying to find his pants.

Then, hallelujah! A phone call! But it was only my editor wanting to know when I'd be able to file my story; the graphics department were waiting to render the map. Unfortunately he didn't know Final Cut Pro either because he used a different system. I asked him if he thought the flashing thing in the cupboard might be malicious and he said, "Probably not," then asked me gently if I was okay out here on my own.

"Apart from not knowing how to shoot, edit or send a story I'm fine."

He agreed I was perfect for the job and wished me luck. I went back to trying to find my pants.

To be honest I don't know how I ended up getting it sorted but sometime through the late afternoon I got something back to Brekky Central. It wasn't much of a story, not much more than a few vox pops of people telling me where they thought the front of Bourke might be – if there was a "back 'o' Bourke" I proposed, there must be a front – but it was something, and it went where it was supposed to go. The system worked, sort of, providing I held my tongue right and didn't upset "the thing" in the cupboard. It was an inglorious start to the trip, but it was a start.

I cooked myself some dinner and crashed early, physically and mentally exhausted. Just as I was fading to black I realised "the thing" was still flashing. I slept with one eye open just in case.

GATHERING DUST

From Bourke I decide to show the Winnebago some gravel to see how it performs, so I take the Hungerford road north to the Queensland border. It isn't one of my better ideas. I ship enough dust to grow vegetables in the back.

There's no worse travelling companion than dust and this rig doesn't handle it well. Wasn't designed for it, way too many orifices, too many cracks, nooks and crannies. In addition there are no mud flaps behind the front drive wheels and the loose stones I'm throwing up smash the unprotected PVC pipes (the campervan's plumbing) and almost close the tailpipe, which oddly comes off at right angles to the road. These issues will need addressing: Australia's got plenty of dirt roads and no shortage of dust.

At the only fuel stop along the way I meet a carload of pig hunters from Melbourne. They've driven all the way on the promise of access to a property, only to find their contact has scarpered and left them with nowhere to hunt. They're a forlorn-looking bunch dressed in black denim jeans and red flannelette shirts and they're moping around the roadhouse waiting for a lifeline to save them doing the whole trip in vain.

On the back of their ute they've got cages full of the ugliest dogs I've ever seen. The group's default spokesman tells me they're wolfhound crosses. He doesn't say what they're crossed with but my guess is a gorilla.

The speaker is a small man with big tattoos. As he talks he

checks out everything else going on around us. He reminds me of someone networking the room at an Attention Deficit Disorder conference. Only when he works out I'm making television does he focus on what I'm saying long enough to offer their services for a story. But doing a pig hunt without pigs doesn't really appeal.

"Why not?"

"Sorry mate. I'm only shooting attractive people. It's for Sunrise."

His eyes widen for a moment as I imagine he considers slitting my throat, before deciding I must be joking.

"We could fake a hunt," he says hopefully.

"Do you use guns or knives?"

"Just knives. And the dogs."

"That's going to be a bit hard to trick up, don't you think? Which one of your mates wants to be the pig?"

His mates wander away with their heads down, suddenly no longer interested in the conversation. The speaker spits his disgust and follows.

Later I get chatting to the local policeman at Eulo – one of those friendly country coppers that are a credit to the breed – and I mention seeing the piggers at Hungerford, a hundred and thirty kilometres south.

"Were they covered in tatts? Three guys one girl?" he asks.

"That sounds about right."

"Yeah, we're watching that lot."

I didn't think they were up to much more than what they said but I find it interesting how everyone knows what everyone else is up to in the country. You think you're on your own out here, but you're not.

I make a beeline for the coast and in Toowoomba I meet the first real eccentric of the trip. He's a retailer with so much stock piled up in his store you can barely make your way down some of the aisles, while others are blocked off completely. Entire rooms are impenetrable. When I arrive one of his regulars is buying some pots and pans, but she waits at the entrance while the shop owner fetches the goods.

"You don't go in?" I ask her.

"No. Might never get out," she laughs, but she's only half-joking.

Although it looks like a disorganised mess he knows exactly where everything is. At one stage something falls to the floor at the other end of the shop and he identifies the object by the sound alone. I point to a random section of the mess, no more than an indistinct jumble of boxes and assorted merchandise looking much like the rest, and ask him when he last had a look in there.

"I was in there yesterday," he says, using the term "in" like you'd describe diving in a swimming pool, "looking for that blue handled jug." He points to it sitting on a box behind us, then pivots and points to a spot about two metres further along, "But in the end I found it over there."

He's a small man with a round face and he looks like he could only ever have been a retailer or an accountant, and he answers my questions without apology. If he's aware his retail practices are in any way unusual he's not letting on.

I ask him how our shopping habits have changed in the fifty-odd years he's been in retail and his answer surprises me.

"The microwave oven's made the biggest difference."

"To the way we cook," he continues when I look puzzled. Of course: one of his main lines is microwave-proof plastic containers.

"What about credit cards?"

"Yes, yes, they've pretty much done away with lay-bys," he concedes. "But it's the microwave..."

I ask him where he keeps his merchant card machine and he points it out on the floor, blending in with all the other crap down there. There is also a cash register sitting on what is presumably the front counter, though both are all but buried under piles of junk.

He produces a long, thin object from somewhere and asks me if I know what it is.

"It's a plastic wrap cutter. It's my biggest seller," he says in the same matter-of-fact way he delivers his other nuggets of retail gold. I'm not sure which is the more absurd: the fact that a plastic wrap cutter is his best seller or the fact that he accepts that as a reasonable thing. Not even the Monty Python team could have drawn a character so fine.

He's seventy-one years old and still single, having lived with his mother till she died a few years ago, aged ninety. I ask if he's still up for it if the right girl came along.

"Well, I do have a house on the Gold Coast. And several blocks of flats here in town. And a tennis court." Then he grins the wild and crazy grin of a man making a pitch for a wife on national television.

I say I'll nominate him if they ever get around to doing "Retailer Finds a Wife" and move on to the next town, thinking I've captured a rare bird on video. It's not till I sit down to edit the story the next day that I realise I've buggered up the audio and may not be able to use his quotes. I almost weep.

MELTDOWN

Mother Theresa and I have become a fixture on the waterfront at Hervey Bay. Mother Theresa's the name I've given the Winnebago because my sponsors like the idea of the campervan developing a personality. When they asked me why I chose that name I told them it was a reference to the amount of action she was seeing: almost two weeks into the trip and not an orgy or a "ritual disembowelment" in sight*. I don't think my answer put them at ease any.

* Quote from the first in the ***RED IN THE CENTRE*** series: ***The Australian Bush Through Urban Eyes***, taken from a letter Rover Australia sent to the Nine Network back in my Today Show days, after I returned from Cape York one car short and one car a bit the worse for wear.

Anyway, I'm hanging out here because I'm having another techno meltdown. I originally called in to get Mother a quick dust proofing, but then the little men in the computer starting calling me names and making fun of me again.

That's what my Final Cut Pro guru imagines when he's got technical issues: that there's a little man in the computer who just needs understanding. He told me this without a trace of embarrassment, I might add. I didn't tell him I was a trained psychiatric nurse who used to get paid to look after people saying exactly the same stuff. No, my guru probably eats Hershey bars for breakfast and gets paid a great deal more for talking to the little men in the machine than I ever did for convincing the lunatics they didn't exist.

Though he still can't help me because he's on holidays now. He got back from America and promptly disappeared again. It's getting harder to remain objective about this. But what I do is go on local radio and put out a call for an FCP expert. Hallelujah, I find one lurking under a rock just above the high tide mark.

I guess we always knew at school that one day the nerds would get the power, that there'd be payback for all the taunting and grief inflicted upon them. Well, it's happened. Now uncool is very cool and the geeks have inherited the earth.

My FCP guy is so good I want to download him. He's more than happy to help. At least that's what he tells me at the beginning. Then I start ringing him. Hourly. No sooner does he solve one problem for me than I ring with another. Before long I'm visiting him at his work. I get anxious and fret if I can't see him. It's like the early stages of a romance only the relief is better. In the end I have to break it off before he reports me for stalking.

One of the advantages of temporary insanity is you don't really notice it yourself; it just feels right for you at the time. For example, I'm almost certain I walked into the water fully clothed at the end of the last segment I just shot. Luckily most people take no notice of people doing bizarre things for television cameras, these days.

Yesterday at Munduberra I had a thoughtful, intelligent entomologist stick his head in a small tent full of flies and mug it for the camera*. Took about point-five of a second to convince him to do it; in fact I think it was his idea.

He told me there were fifteen thousand flies in the tent so naturally I asked him how he knew.

"We count the legs and divide by six."

A nice, television-friendly grab. He was good talent, the entomologist. Knew how to keep his message clear and simple. Make a joke or two along the way. Had a friendly face and a big smile he used a lot.

"We breed good bugs to control the bad bugs," he told me. "To give farmers a natural alternative to chemical pest control."

As well as the flies he showed me maggots (the nursery), ladybugs, lacewings and wasps so tiny you could barely see them.

"How do you send these little ones out to the farmers?"

"In these," he said, holding up a plastic drink cup, complete with clear plastic lid, "ten thousand at a time."

* See photo, colour section one, page 5, top.

"Doesn't look very scientific; that's a take away coffee cup, isn't it?"

"Here we call them Aphytus rearing cylinders," he laughs.

"How do they get the insects out of the cup and distributed evenly?"

"We put ten pieces of paper in the cup which the wasps naturally settle on at roughly a thousand per strip. Then all the farmer has to do is walk through his orchard spreading the strips of paper about, and the wasps fly off and set to work on the Red Scale bug. Exactly what they were born to do."

A clever man, no doubt. And he'll play in a tray of maggots if you ask him. (He draws the line at eating them. *Of course* I asked: that's my job.)

Meanwhile I'm still snookered on the IT front. Word has got out in the caravan park that I'm having a breakdown. A woman just brought me some home made cookies and cake. They were very nice. Another woman sent her young boy along to say hello. I ate him as well. When he didn't return the lady at the front office came asking if I'd seen him. I told her yes and to keep sending them through, I'm going to need more where that came from to get me through this.

On the way out of town I call in to the shopping centre to buy a few supplies. It's there I get the call from my producer and my worst fears are confirmed: the audio on my retailer story is unfit for broadcast and I have to do a voice-over to salvage enough to make the segment work. Now – in the shopping centre car park.

While I'm doing it a woman with two small children comes up

to say hello. I grab one of her children and eat him on the spot. I motion for her to pass me the other one but she grabs the girl and runs.

Three days at Hervey Bay is supposed to chill you out but I feel strangely unsatisfied. As I drive out of town I comb the streets looking for something else to eat.

GENTLE SOULS

In north Queensland I meet a man who hunts luminous mushrooms in the rainforest. They bloom when it rains and he likes walking through the forest with a torch at night and seeing the mushrooms sprouting. When he was younger he used to strip naked and paint himself with the luminescence.

"They secrete a kind of gel you can rub on your skin and give yourself a visible glow in the dark," he says.

I wonder out loud why he'd even think to do such a thing.

"Oh, I used to take my girlfriends out into the forest and paint them as well," he says laughing. I gather he wasn't referring to their portraits.

He's a quiet, sensitive sort of man who I imagine has a natural inclination to blend into the background. He lives and works in a small country town and it's unlikely his fellow residents know of his nocturnal hobby, much less his predilection for glow in the dark sex romps when he was younger.

He's lived in the rainforest all his life and his interest in its ways is partly natural, partly circumstantial.

"I had a car accident when I was in my teens" he tells me, "and spent a lot of time walking slowly through the rainforest on crutches, recuperating. I learned a lot about the forest then."

The mushrooms in question are *Mycena chlorophanos*, found east of the ranges from Sydney to Cape York. Typically they grow on rotting vegetation in rainforest habitat and put on quite a show when conditions are favourable. My man doesn't care to know the scientific name, but he does agree they can be spectacularly bright.

"I knew an old dairy farmer who told me he once wrote a letter by the light of a mushroom. Just held it over the paper and the glow was enough to see what he was writing."

It's too dry for the mushrooms while I'm there but he takes me for a walk anyway and identifies the flora and fauna we see with the awe of a child.

"Look at that," he says in wonder several times over this highlight or that. "Isn't it beautiful?"

"And if man's not careful we'll lose all this," he says wistfully at one point.

But I wonder which is under the greatest threat: the rainforest or men like him.

I met another man in the same vicinity who quit the city when he was twenty-four to come and live on a two hundred acre block in the tropics. He bought the land because he couldn't afford a smaller block closer to town. Now he's grateful for the privacy.

"I think people who spend all their lives in the city are crazy," he says, grinning. "My brother came to visit me a few years back, with his missus, and they stayed one night. Couldn't stand the insects and the wildlife. So they booked into a motel in town, with air conditioning."

It's hardly surprising. His hand-built shack has no walls on two sides and the toilet and shower are open and positioned to take full advantage of the view. In addition there's an enormous bird feeder alive with parrots and honeyeaters in the middle of the space where the northeast wall would be. So if you were sitting on the throne the effect would be like looking across the lounge room through an aviary to a pretty green valley in the middle distance. A tranquil meditation for a man living on his own, no doubt, but I daresay a mortifying experience for his brother's wife.

His furnishings, too, are modest and practical at best, and the modern telephone handset looks strangely out of place fixed to a rough-hewn hardwood post. There are no feminine touches in sight.

He's a man of about sixty with a Mexican handlebar moustache, and he's wearing a fourth-day shirt and jeans with no shoes. He smokes roll-your-own cigarettes and rarely has one out of his mouth for the time I'm there. And he smiles readily as he talks in a Yugoslavian accent that twenty-five years of solitude has done little to diminish.

"I was a taxi driver in the city before I came here. And I went back for a visit about five, no ten years ago rather," he says, surprising himself to remember how long ago it was, "but that was a bit crazy and I promised myself I'd never go anywhere near the city again.

"In Sydney, on the harbour bridge I did a u-ey because I tried to get off the bridge and kept ending up back on it. They all tooted their horns but I wanted to go to Liverpool."

These days they'd have probably shot him.

It's hard to imagine how he fills his time but I suspect he spends a goodly portion of it watching the birds.

"They cost me thirty dollars a week for feed," he says, scattering some seed on the feeder, "but they're worth it." A cock King Parrot comes in to land quite close and for a moment in time man and bird consider one another, the parrot turning its head to one side to weigh up the threat. Satisfied there is none the bird begins feeding and breaks the tableau.

He keeps his own food suspended in a hammock with tin plate barriers at either end to stop the rats eating it. The plates have holes through their centres and spin freely on the ropes so the rats can't get any purchase to clamber over them, but he has a rabbit trap set and waiting on the other side of the plates in case one does learn the trick. I imagine it also discourages him from feeling around for a midnight snack in the middle of the night.

Though I don't expect he would relish killing a rat. While we're chatting he's been quietly killing March Flies and adding them to a small pile of them he has on the wooden floor.

"For the ants," he tells me. "They like them."

He also keeps native bees, though not for any reason you might think. He opens one of his hives and shows me the bees and lets me taste the honey. It's watery by comparison to commercial honey and almost too sweet to eat. But he doesn't eat it anyway.

"I don't rob the bees because I worry they won't have enough honey for themselves," he tells me. "I've got a lot of bees here to feed."

I tell him he's a kind-hearted man and he enjoys the compliment.

"I feel like a Buddhist monk walking along with a branch," he says with a big smile, "sweeping the ants from his path so he doesn't step on them."

I smile back and then look across at my guide – the luminous mushroom man who's brought me here – to see him nodding approvingly. And I really can't imagine two gentler souls.

COMFORTABLE

"Man is not complete until he is married and then he is finished."

That little gem came from next door. It's probably a chestnut so old it does the rounds with every generation but I'd never heard it before. One can learn many profound things at my next-door-neighbours' caravan.

Like how they always travel with an icemaker, for instance. And a bread-maker. And a portable washing machine. And probably a drier as well though at the time I was still struggling to comprehend the washing machine and couldn't conceive the possibility enough to ask.

"Only cost me two hundred dollars. Gotta be comfortable," he says with a knowing smile I don't quite reciprocate. For the uninitiated, every caravan park in the country has washing facilities if not bread- and icemakers, and they'd need to do sixty-odd loads of washing before they started saving on cost.

He's a likeable, big-bellied man with a ruddy round face full of white stubble. His wife is strong-boned and healthy and looks a good match for him. Together they've been towing a pop top caravan around the country behind their little 4x4 since they retired a year or so ago. They spend a couple of months at a time away from home.

When they're not on the road they live in a sixty square house for just the two of them and he's got a shed "like you wouldn't believe". His hobby is collecting old American cars and he has "six babies waiting back home right now".

They wouldn't consider themselves wealthy people, just good old Aussies who've worked hard enough to enjoy their retirement with a few of life's creature comforts.

I quiz them gently on their views on climate change and it seems both are cautious believers. He thinks the seas will rise but not as much as "they say". She believes overpopulation is the culprit "right there". Neither sees their consumerism as part of the problem. They do what they can to recycle and buy green when there's an option, providing it doesn't impact on their lifestyle.

"What else can we do? I still have to run me cars, don't I?" He becomes far more passionate when discussing the high cost of oil than the possibility of the world ending. And she loves their grandchildren, of course, but can't really see how anything they're doing might have an impact on the world we'll be leaving them.

I'm left feeling as though their approach is representative of mainstream Australia and it worries me. They are decent people living life the way they've grown up believing they're entitled to live it and nobody can blame them for that. *But do we really need all this stuff?* Isn't it bad enough that we all want McMansions and new cars and more toys, now we expect the same creature comforts when we go camping, for Christ's sake? Surely if we all keep pursuing our right to be comfortable like this we'll run out of resources, never mind whatever climate change will or won't do to the world.

Later in the trip I meet a different style of comfortable. He comes in the form of a man who is living in a Gympie caravan park because Cyclone Larry blew away his North Queensland home. But 'trailer trash' or not this man dresses with a sense of pride. According to his girlfriend he always dresses well. She told me he gets photographed all the time and once even got dragged into a Japanese wedding to pose with the bride and groom, who must have been intrigued by this diminutive man in the natty cowboy outfit*.

When I first saw him he was standing in the rain outside the park toilets wearing a cowboy hat and holding an umbrella over

* See photo, colour section one, page 4, bottom right.

his head. Though her caravan was no more than twenty metres away he was waiting to walk her back. Chivalry cut a dashing figure even in the wet.

We started talking and I decided to interview him the next day, but the video camera was too moisture-laden to operate – a lesson there for young players like me – so I had to settle for a still photograph.

Just before I took the photo I went into the toilets looking for a hand dryer to dry the video camera and got abused by another of the park's residents. Not about anything worth crossing words over: just a bloke full of anger looking for somewhere to spend it.

When I found no hand dryer I came out and broke the news about the camera to my dapper friend. If he was disappointed to be missing out on an interview on national television he didn't let it show. The contrast between him and the bloke in the toilet was stark.

He rolled a cigarette and told me about their home Larry destroyed without once complaining about their ill-fortune, instead concentrating on the wonderful things they'd seen travelling down from Far North Queensland. I listened in awe of these unassuming people, and when I gave them my book and CD they humbled me with their gratitude.

Before I left he came up to Mother Theresa and gave me a smooth piece of smoked quartz for luck, telling me how I must put it in salt water or bury it in earth for a time to cleanse it so his energy was erased and mine could be adopted.

"But you must believe," he said. "Believe it will bring you luck and it will."

I must have looked bemused because then he said, "I may not look like I've got much, but I'm comfortable." Then he touched the brim of his hat and was gone.

CITY SLICKER

Not everyone in the country is happy to see you. A few would rather we city types kept to our patch and left them alone.

I was trying to find a couple of cameleers I knew were on a stock route south of Blackall, but I took a wrong turn and got bogged in soft sand. We'd spoken via satellite phone and they'd given me directions, but somehow I lost my way and found myself on one of those tracks that promise the world then deteriorate too quickly to let you turn around. At that point you have no option but to carry on as fast as you dare and hope you reach the other shore before you sink. I never made it. And Mother Theresa's got little wheels and a big arse so I was well and truly stuck*.

But it was no big deal. I was no more than a kilometre from the nearest farmhouse and had plenty of water and food on board. I wasn't worried.

It was late afternoon so I walked back to the farmhouse to raise some help but there was nobody home. A handful of chooks and

* See photo, colour section two, page 1, top.

a few working dogs made up the welcoming committee and there were no fresh tyre tracks anywhere to be seen. I'm not suggesting any black tracking skills here: the cameleers told me they'd had good rain in the past forty-eight hours so it was easy enough to figure out.

I knew someone would be home sooner rather than later if only to feed the animals, but that still might be a day or two away. I borrowed a shovel and walked back to the rig.

It wasn't much of a shovel, but then I was only half-hearted about digging myself out so we got on fine. I cleared a bit of sand from the front wheels, stuffed some bark and a couple of sticks under them and tried to rock it out, but that only dug me in further till I was sitting on the undercarriage.

Dusk sneaked up on me while I wasn't looking so I stopped pretending to save myself and lit a fire. I opened a good bottle and cooked dinner and I've paid big money for less in the city. I slept like a pig and woke to a perfect Australian morning, with magpies chortling and kangaroos bounding towards the rising sun as it filtered through the eucalypts. It could have been a scene straight from a feel-good Aussie soap opera. Except for the empty wine bottle by the campfire, of course, and the rough head staggering out of the Winnebago.

I decided it was time to get serious about extracting myself from the bog. While there was still no threat to my well being, I did have a deadline to meet and nothing short of your untimely demise is good enough excuse for television, and even then it will be expected you had the presence of mind to film yourself dying (which I had been doing, I might add, just in case).

I contacted my cameleers again and half-jokingly suggested they wander over and pull me out with their team, which would have made good television. Instead they gave me contact numbers for a couple of the nearby stations. Camels may be beasts of burden but obviously they don't stoop to roadside assist.

(By the way, I'd already tried calling the Winnebago Roadside Assist number on the windscreen sticker that guaranteed "Anywhere Anytime Support", but apparently my particular dilemma fell outside those narrow parameters and wasn't covered.)

So I called and left messages at both stations then made another trip to the farmhouse nearby to no avail. I was busying myself stalking some kangaroos for a camera shot when a return call came through. It sounded prickly from the outset.

"Did you leave a message for us?" she started.

So I told her my situation and asked her if there was any chance of getting someone to mosey on over in a 4x4 and give me a tow out.

To be fair she didn't deny me help, and I had no problem with the men being busy till after smoko when she "*might* be able to get someone to come". But the level of sanctimony was palpable.

"You wouldn't know where the farmer here is, by any chance?" I asked her. "Or his town number if he's got one?"

"No, I don't think he'd appreciate getting caught up in this mess."

And while I could hardly miss her tone I carried on politely explaining I didn't see it as a mess so much as an opportunity to make some fun television and show the town off in a good light in the process. But she was having none of it.

"Oh no, we wouldn't be interested in that," she said.

Then she went on to tell me how much of an imposition it was when people "doing what they shouldn't be doing" caused trouble for country people and I could stand no more. I told her not to worry about it I'd sort it out myself.

"No, you stay put," she told me in her bossiest best. "I'll send someone when I can."

The prospect of another sermon when help arrived was too painful to contemplate. I picked up the shovel and got stuck in. Three hours later I had the old girl dug out and jacked up with logs under each of the front wheels. Driving her out was about the sweetest experience I've had in recent times, matched only by the call I made to the station to tell Madam Bossy thanks but no thanks, I wouldn't need her help after all.

Later that morning the other station owner I'd rung rang back to make sure I was out and safe. I told him I was and relayed the essence of the story to him.

"Yes, she's an inspirational lady," he said tactfully.

Maybe so, and she was quite likely a damned good one to have around, as well. But I'm too stubborn to take help from the self-righteous. I'd rather perish waiting for grace.

I found my cameleers ten minutes away; I'd missed them by a fork in the road. They were a couple in their forties with smiling, tanned faces who'd taken to wandering the country with five camels and a little pink wagon three months earlier. Their kids had grown up and left so they decided to do it before they got too old.

"We just walk along, seeing the country, talking to the people," the man of the team told me. He had an impish grin that he used to good effect making whatever he said sound cheeky. The woman didn't say much, just chimed in occasionally with a laughing remark; but she was always in the mix even when she was tending the camels over by the way. It was like spending time with a couple of close siblings.

"How's the reception from the farmers?" I had to ask.

"They're great, most of them. 'Stay as long as you want, take what you need'. You get the odd one not so keen. Had one old girl lately stop and ask me if the camels were carrying ticks. Didn't think quick enough: should've told her yeah, got plenty. How many do you want?"

I wondered if his "old girl" and mine were one and the same.

I left the cameleers and moved on. About an hour down the road the last piece of the puzzle fell into place when the absent farmer called me. He asked me three questions: What happened? Where are you now? And what were you doing there in the first place?

I answered his questions and told him I borrowed a shovel but put it back, filled the hole as best I could and closed all the gates behind me. I didn't tell him not to worry about me coming back anytime soon. I figured his concern wasn't for my welfare anyway.

NO SNAKES

On a stinking hot day in the middle of the flattest, driest plain in the Northern Territory I happened upon a cyclist*. He was riding around the world and had already covered much of Europe and Asia, and had New Zealand and the Americas in his sights. Once he got through Australia unscathed, of course.

He had the wiry build of many cyclists and seemed glad to be stopped for a chat, though his first response when I told him I had a television interview in mind was that his English wasn't good enough. I convinced him it was and shot a highly amusing piece with him then and there on the side of the road, with him showing me all his equipment with great style and ceremony.

Then I realised I'd forgotten to press the record button – common beginner's mistake – and had to do it over again. The second interview, as always, was much inferior to the first. Nothing beats spontaneity for catching the essence of a personality.

What I did catch, though, was that he was a twenty-five year old man from the Basque country in northern Spain and he was a newly qualified mechanical engineer. He had a girlfriend back home who he communicated with using Skype – mobile phone was "too much expensive" in Australia, hear, hear – and he used an impressive portable solar charger to keep his phone and Ipod charged.

He carried ten one litre bottles of water with him in the desert, the usual lightweight sleeping and cooking gear, a few clothes and a little green mascot called Pokoyo that looked like Elvis

* See photo, colour section one, page 4, top right.

gone wrong to me. He assured me Pokoyo was very famous back in Spain.

He was proud of a little odometer mounted on his handlebars that showed he'd averaged seventeen kilometres an hour for the day and covered over a hundred and fifty kilometres. Ditto a tiny bell that wasn't loud enough to raise alarm beyond about a metre, but seemed to please its owner.

But the best part of the interview was when I asked him about his sleeping arrangements.

"Free camping," he said, gesturing at the roadside.

"Aren't you worried about snakes?"

"No snakes."

"Are you sure about that?"

"No snakes, no spiders, I am sure," he replied with some conviction, though smiling broadly now.

"You know they'll crawl into your sleeping bag in the desert, looking for warmth?"

"No, there are no snakes," he insisted, still grinning. "I am lucky man."

I liked his attitude. How else was he going to sleep amongst them but in total denial?

In fact Australia has eighteen of the twenty most venomous snakes in the world, with the Inland Taipan* and the Common

* Later in the trip I saw a large Inland Taipan and noticed for the first time the coffin-shaped nose used to distinguish the Taipan from the Brown. I hasten to add I only got close enough to see this because the snake was already dead.

Brown right up the top of the list. Despite these realities there are very few fatalities from snakebite, with the vast majority occurring either by accident – ie stepping on the snake – or alcohol-fuelled misadventure. One of the main reasons for this is most of Australia's snakes have poor injection systems, relying on external grooves on the fangs to transport the venom to the prey instead of the hollow-fanged "hypodermic" system found in many offshore snakes.

For your peace of mind the treatment of choice these days – and I had this confirmed at the Alice Springs Reptile Park, which kindly provided a Mulga Snake for me to film for the cyclist segment – is to immobilise the limb and keep the patient as calm as possible till an antivenom can be administered.

This would prove no mean feat if you're alone at the time of the strike since most of us don't carry antivenom in our pockets. Then you'd be faced with the decision of whether you wait and tough it out, hoping you didn't cop enough venom to kill you, or exert energy seeking medical assistance knowing in the process you'd spread the venom through your system and give it every chance of maximum effect anyway.

The other dilemma you face is how much time you've got, with some venom taking much longer to act than others. The ranger at the Reptile Park told me about being struck recently and thought he was fine for about five minutes then was unconscious within ten. Luckily there was help nearby and a hospital just up the road.

"It's not pleasant," he assured me. "If you imagine cutting yourself with a knife then burning the open wound with a soldering iron that's about what a Mulga Snake bite feels like.

"Then once you've been given the antivenom your body has to deal with this massive dose of horse protein as well as the venom.

"It takes days before you're right. Weeks, even. I don't recommend it as Outback experiences go."

Of course none of this would have been of interest to my Spanish cyclist since he was a non-believer.

I gave him a copy of my book and a bottle of cold water and wished him luck. Then I put my arm over his shoulder and pointed to the laser-flat horizon at the far extremity of the most barren piece of country the Territory has to offer.

"See that out there. What do you think lies beyond?"

"Nothing," he said wisely. "There's nothing there, only more of the same."

"Ah, but that's where you're wrong. Over that horizon is a beautiful oasis with palm trees and shade and cold beer for a thirsty traveller."

"I wish," he said following my gaze.

The last I saw of him he was a speck in the distance, pedalling his bike towards a well-earned beer at the oasis in this snake-free land of ours.

AT LARGE

Just north of Alice Springs is a roadhouse overlooked by an enormous blackfella statue perched up on a hill. It's twelve metres tall and set back from the road aways, and at first glance it's hard to determine whether it's the tackiest roadside attraction you've ever seen or the most authentic. Certainly you wonder what sort of mind could possibly conceive such a thing in these politically correct times, and you call in. Anmatjere Man has done his job.

"Yeah, this is Anmatjere country," the proprietor tells me, pronouncing the name of the aboriginal mob *ummudjera*. "And when tourists ask me 'Why have you got a blackfella on the hill?' I say, 'Well don't you think a porpoise or a Minke Whale would look a bit out of place out here?'"

The proprietor is a small, bald man who wears glasses on the end of his nose. He's also bigger than his physical dimensions by about the power of five. I have a theory that a personality will expand to fill the available space and this guy's a case in point. He's been running roadhouses for most of his sixty years and he swears like a wharfie, which makes him difficult talent to interview for mainstream television. Indeed, when he finishes the previous offering we all laugh because he's managed to string two sentences together without swearing once.

As well as Anmatjere Man on the hill he's also commissioned the sculptor to build a woman and child, a job he's now well into. She's an imposing structure and the child comes up to her waist*.

* See photo, colour section one, page 7, top.

They're solidly made of chicken wire shaped around heavy-duty square steel framing, and soon they'll be ready for the cement render finish coat. They've consulted the local women on issues like positioning and colour and it was they who determined she should stand on the flat below her man above.

"We were going to put her up on the hill with the man, but the women told me she couldn't go up there because he's got a spear, he's hunting."

"'You stand her up where she is, old man,' they told me. So now I've got a nine metre garden gnome in my back yard. With a kid."

They're fine-looking statues and I compliment the sculptor on his flair for womanly curves.

"I've done some research over the years." He grins. "And the Anmatjere women all seem to approve of her."

"What about the men? Were they happy with the big fella's proportions?"

"Yeah, sometimes they walk around boasting, you know, 'I'm Anmatjere Man.' But I gave him a loin cloth so we didn't offend anyone."

Not that causing offence is a big concern for the proprietor. He's had a party trick incorporated into the design of the woman statue.

"We had her plumbed in," he tells me. "True! And it's a good stream, too. So you can stand underneath her and get your picture taken having a golden shower."

Naturally I video it for my segment but it gets edited out by the

Thought Police back at Sunrise*. Europe, the hub of the cultured world, may be full of pissing statues, but we won't tolerate such coarseness here.

Meanwhile the stories get more outrageous with every beer.

In a yard outside the tavern he's got a pet wedge-tailed eagle called Bozo** that the tourists love to photograph.

"We used to keep him behind sheets of reo***, you know, with the big squares in it?" he says, shaping his hands into a square the size of a house brick. "And these tourists were out there one time with their little dog, and Bozo reached through the wire and grabbed him through the eye and pulled him into his cage and into him. Had him gutted in thirty seconds flat!

"Well, there was yelling and screaming, the woman was wailing, and the bloke was demanding I go in and get their dog back and I said, 'I'll tell you what, I'll open the gate and you go in and see if you can get the dog off him.'

"But I gave them a postcard and thanked them for feeding him."

And while it's impossible to know just how much is poetic licence and how much is truth, it doesn't matter. He's an entertaining man who'll amuse you if you let him.

He's also more spiritual than you'd imagine a foul-mouthed,

* Merry band of good taste arbiters whose members made themselves conspicuous by their absence whenever I wanted to question an editing decision.

** See photo, colour section one, page 6, bottom.

*** Steel wire re-inforcement for concrete foundations.

outback publican to be. He recently hosted some Catholic nuns and closed the bar to hold a church service. Wrote the service times on a VB sign and put it out the front. Tourists stopped to take pictures of the sign, unaware of the seriousness behind the contradiction.

"Yeah, when the nuns left we gave them an envelope full of money and told them they had to spend it on drinking and gambling, but they sent us a receipt for the full amount," he says, with a perfect mix of disappointment and satisfaction.

I ask if he'll be happy once he's got the woman and child finished and the Anmatjere family complete.

"Nah, then I'm gonna build a big Rainbow Serpent out the front."

"How big?"

"About a kilometre. Going in and out of the ground. I want to put some spirit back in to the land, you know?"

"They're a good mob, the Anmatjere. They do great art, more colourful than a lot of the other stuff, happier. I tell 'em I want to be buried over the road where they all sit and talk.

"'You can't be buried there, old man,' they say. 'We sit there.'

"I say 'I know, that's why I want to be buried there: so I can reach out of the ground and grab a can from you.'"

Footnote: I called in on the second lap and Anmatjere woman and child were finished, but work on the Serpent had been postponed in favour of building a new bar. Fair enough.

TOO MUCH

Darwin at this time of year is no place for the faint-hearted.

When I arrive to do the live cross there's a young man with his pants around his ankles, asleep on the footpath in the middle of the city. I try to wake him but he isn't responding. He's got underpants on so the sight isn't overly obscene, but it's hard not to imagine how he might have ended up in that state of undress. He has a little Freddy Mercury moustache and a pleasant, boyish face. I don't really want to think about what he might have been up to while I'm trying to exchange pleasantries with Kochie and Mel back in the studio. He opens one eye slightly, but I can't say for sure he sees me before he closes it again. I leave him to his business and get on with mine.

The live link point is a tiny back corner room of the Qantas building that also houses the ABC studios where I began my television career twenty-odd years before. Back then my star was on the rise and anything was possible. Now I was standing in the side alley urging a garbage truck out of the way so I could do an entertainment report on a movie I never saw, with a young man asleep with his pants down not fifteen metres away. What a stellar career it's been.

The night before I'd attended the pre-screening party for the premier of the movie Australia, to get some vision for the show.

"Just get some Monte colour," came the direction.

So I trotted along to get some Monte colour, whatever that meant. But unlike the Darwin I used to know, most of the guests were too intent on staying sober before the screening to give me a decent vox pop. In the end I got the women talking about the male lead's shower scene (which had been previewed on the talk shows) and gathered half a dozen lively but inoffensive quotes about what constitutes a good sex scene in the cinema. Unfortunately the Thought Police struck again and cut the juice out of it – in my biased opinion, of course – and I was left wondering why I bothered. But at least now I knew what colour they meant: beige.

Anyway, when it came time to do my piece to camera in the morning I didn't have much enthusiasm for it. The link point offered exactly two backdrops and pants boy featured heavily in one of them, and it was already too hot to be standing in the sun. When it was my turn to review the movie the best I could come up with was, "A masterpiece, every frame I saw," which was a misleading piece of glibberish I'm not the least bit proud of.

But Darwin at this time of year can make a man do silly things. I did a photo shoot for the local newspaper and let the photographer snap me holding an umbrella. I don't know why I let her do that when I refused to hold an umbrella for photographers back when I *was* still a weatherman (my futile protest against their lack of originality). The photo in the paper the next day makes me feel sick.

And Darwin at this time of year is like living in a sauna. It's a thousand degrees by eight o'clock in the morning and if you can afford the indulgence it's not completely ridiculous to be drinking cold beer by mid-morning and glaze your way through the afternoon. It's tempting since I've got Mother Theresa booked in for a number of service calls, but it becomes problematic turning up drunk to collect your car. Most workshops don't approve of you crawling in the back for a sleep before you drive away.

And in Darwin at this time of year the cicadas are loud enough to swamp your thoughts and vivid green frogs shock you from the toilet bowl and turbocharged flora and fauna invades your home and every afternoon the clouds promise but don't deliver and the awful sound of domestic violence is never more than a beautiful sunset away and the swelter continues getting worse every year or are we all just getting older Christ any more of this and surely I'll lose my grip.

No, Darwin at this time of year is no place for the faint-hearted. It's too hot, too harsh and altogether too much. As a younger man it was all new and exciting and I could pretend it wasn't happening, but these days I'm not such a good actor.

I finish the live cross and it leaves me empty like television sometimes can when you weren't happy with your performance. I'm pissed off with myself for trying to fit in with the froth and bubble of the show I'm working for, and I'm pissed off with the faceless, nameless kids now preventing me being the master of my own destiny. I feel old and irrelevant.

Walking back to Mother Theresa I notice pants boy has got himself up and moved on, and I decide that's a very good idea.

FRONTIER TOWN

"When I first came here thirty years ago," says the storyteller, eyes twinkling, "I remember a bloke coming into the pub wearing a pair of six shooters. He was showing off, trying to quick draw and shoot some bottles off a ledge, but when he drew his guns to fire only one came out and the other one blew half his foot off!"

We all laugh. It's not a story from the wild west of the United States, but from Wyndham, Australia. Wyndham is like Darwin without the creature comforts. You can't stay sane in the heat. It corrupts your judgement. You drink too much. Or you don't drink enough. Either way it's no wonder people are cross-threaded up here.

I've just spent a full day in it getting waylaid chasing a story without an ending. It's about an old publican who died back in the days before refrigeration, and got buried in haste with the keys to the pub in his pocket. So the ever-pragmatic locals exhumed his body and retrieved the keys. But while everybody agrees it's probably true and the measures undertaken (sorry) were entirely justifiable, nobody knows much more than that.

I even looked in the cemetery most likely to hold his remains – there are five cemeteries in Wyndham – but got sidetracked by the decorative graves, which have black and tan border stones, like Coral Snakes. It was a Shire initiative, apparently, though I can't rightly imagine how the concept was sold at the council meeting.

Before that I drank a toast to a soul whose ashes were buried under the tiled floor of the pub, was shown pens in the croc farm where the previous owner's ashes were scattered, and saw an enormous crocodile head in a bloke's freezer*, looking strangely at home next to the ice cream and frozen chickens. Or maybe I was going the same way as the locals? In any case it seemed everywhere I looked led to the grave in one form or another, but not the grave I wanted.

And now I'm sitting around with half a dozen hard men and true, drinking beer and discussing a criminal with a household name who's known personally to these guys, who was convicted of a murder they are certain he didn't commit. Their arguments are simple and compelling: he was too thorough, too determined to do only half the job (if he had a mind to do it in the first place, which they don't believe). It's not the natural bias of mates I'm hearing here, but the matter-of-fact reasoning of men who talk of death the same way most of us discuss the weather.

Something about this town brings death to the fore. It's as if the harshness of life here won't tolerate any civilised pretence, and survival depends on keeping it very real.

One of my fellow drinkers owns the courthouse. Tells me he bought it because he'd spent enough time inside the building to know it was sound, and he figured crime was about the only real growth industry in town. *And* he gets to contribute to the rental income.

This prompts someone else to tell the story of the two JPs who had to front one another in the courthouse after a particularly boisterous weekend. Being good friends they agreed they'd be lenient with each other.

*See photo, colour section two, page 6, bottom.

"For being out of order on Saturday night I fine you one pound," said the first to the second. They exchanged places.

"I see we've already had a case of this nature before the Court this morning," said the second JP to the first. "I'm doubling the fine to set an example."

And the stories keep coming.

"There was this bloke who wouldn't pay his bills, see," starts another, with the speaker's face so animated you just know it's not going to go well for "this bloke" right from the start. "So the fella he owes money to goes around to his work one day and while he's trying to climb the fence to get away he shoots him fair up the arse."

We laugh. The absurdity of being shot in the bum is too much.

"Stone dead, he was, fell right at his feet," he continues, and for some reason the laughter increases. "So the next night he organised a big bonfire and got all the lads around, then backed the car up to the fire and pulled the body out of the boot and threw him on.

"'That's what happens when you don't pay your bills, boys, he said.' And you could see all these blokes reaching for their wallets ready to sort their debts out on the spot."

These are not your average barroom stories being told here, but then Wyndham's not your average town. It's had a chequered history boasting a gold boom in late 1800s and a thriving meatworks through most of the 1900s, and it's been a deepwater port from the early 1900s to the present, a service currently used for the export of live cattle and zinc and the import of fuel and explosives for the nearby mines. Throw in a modest tourist industry and that's pretty much the sum total of Wyndham's economic story.

Yet even when Wyndham was thriving it was always hot and remote, a town wedged between a brutally beautiful escarpment and gulf full of mangroves and midges and man-eating crocodiles, where only the very hardy or slightly unhinged would choose to live.

"Everyone up here's got something wrong with them," explains Mr Courthouse. "That's why we're all up here."

"What's wrong with you?"

"Everything!" he says, laughing again. "My old lady gave me twenty bucks thirty years ago and told me don't come home till you're a millionaire. I haven't been home since!"

But the place grows on you. And while the rest of the country becomes civilised and towns distance themselves from their colourful beginnings, Wyndham has so far managed to retain its essential rough and ready Kimberley flavour. No doubt it can't resist the tide forever, but I like to think there'll always be somewhere you can go to blow your foot off in this great land of ours.

Footnote: After the incomplete story about the publican went to air a number of people bailed me up to ask me about it. So on the second leg I re-visited Wyndham to retell the story properly. This time I didn't allow myself to get waylaid and traced the yarn back to a mention in a book first published in 1937 called "The Great Australian Loneliness", written by journalist Ernestine Hill, who travelled the country during the 1930s looking at how Australians lived at that time. But apart from sensing a kindred spirit in this author I got no closer to the story than that. The undertaker confirmed that a body would start decomposing within twenty-four hours in normal Wyndham conditions – "the ants and the flies would be all over it" – adding a trace of credibility to the story. But the fact that nobody living could recall the event, and the one surviving resident who was around at the time had no knowledge of it at all, would suggest it might be an urban myth. A good'n, though.

CHARLIE

The town of Broome can sweep you away. Entire lives have been lost up here. People get seduced by the colour of the water and the intoxicating tropical lifestyle and leave it too late to leave. I've always been fond of the place.

Oh, she has her flaws, of course, like all towns. To start with she's a good example of how mainstream Australia is failing the Aborigines every bit as much as they are failing themselves. As Broome prospers the town camps ease into squalor and the signs of a minority group in trouble become more evident*. And she's growing at a rate that appears to be jeopardising her uniqueness; shopping centres and fast-buck tourist developments are going up with no more than lip service being paid to heritage building styles (which I admit were hotch-potch in the first place, but that was part of their charm). But I sense the essence of Broome will always be there for those who want to look beyond the obvious.

I walked into town and bought supplies, then walked back and contacted my cameleer friend from the first Red in the Centre trip. We arranged to meet and I picked him up from one of the pubs, collecting his gear from where he'd stashed it in the scrub on the way out.

"Still living like a blackfella, mate," I said, half in jest.

* To quote Ray Erickson's observations on Broome in his book West of Centre published way back in 1972, "the separate identity and the segregated life of the Aboriginals were as obvious as the colour of their skins: a clear expression of the hypocrisy of a white majority who preach integration and refuse to let it happen."

"Yeah, I reckon I am."

And he wasn't kidding. He was living in a shack on an Aboriginal community to the north of Broome and I gave him a lift home and stayed the night. For once my accommodation was more luxurious than my host's. Quite apart from the rudimentary nature of the living arrangements, he was without protection from the insects and the weather, both of which can get savage in that part of the world.

"Don't know how long I'll last, but the mob here were good enough to let me stay, and I can keep me camels close."

One of his camels had recently been shot with a crossbow and needed a dose of antibiotics, so the first thing we did was attend to this. It was Charlie, the big camel he dug out of the bog in *Through Urban Eyes*, and I felt like I had an attachment to him the way an author forms an attachment to any character he writes about.

"It was a lung shot," the cameleer tells me. "Angled in and meant to kill."

He shows me the tip of the crossbow's bolt that the surgeon removed. It was wooden, with a sliver missing.

"No metal point?"

"No, they use these blunt wooden tips that shatter on impact, just like a hollow point bullet."

"Is that sliver still inside him?"

"I hope not. They're tough animals but they don't do so well with splinters of wood in their guts."

It was dark when we reached him and Charlie was pleased to

see his master, though not so pleased with the injection, going crook in that throaty, gurgling way camels do.

Only once that business had been attended and his master had gone off to find him some hay did he acknowledge my presence, and then only with a faint kiss on the cheek. I like camels for this trait: they kiss you to check you out, unless, of course, they choose to bite or kick you. But mostly I find them even-tempered, intelligent animals. Why anyone would want to shoot one with a crossbow is hard to fathom: for kicks, maybe?

I remember once when I was barely a teenager taking a joy shot at a wallaby, then watching, sickened, as it fell to the ground stone dead. I don't think I've ever fired a weapon for kicks since. I hope Charlie's would-be assassin feels the same way.

In Australia it's legal for anyone over eighteen to own and carry a crossbow without a license in the Northern Territory, South Australia and Western Australia. The eastern states have more rigid controls and usually require the user to be a member of a sporting club before a licence is issued. Because of its concealable size, the pistol crossbow is strictly controlled in *all* states and territories, but policing *any* crossbow laws is difficult because the weapons make almost no noise when fired.

And camels are big business in Broome. Since about the early eighties camel tours have been operating for the tourists to enjoy sunset rides along Cable Beach. It's one of the things you do in Broome, as mandatory as watching a movie in the open-air cinema and having a coldie at the Roey (Roebuck Bay Hotel). Naturally in that time there's been some healthy competition between the tour operators, occasionally even not so healthy, and while my cameleer doesn't get involved in the local camel politics he does have his suspicions about who might have shot Charlie.

"Yeah, I probably should have gone to the police, but I got talked out of it," he says, laying out only the bare tracks for his train of thought. "Maybe it was a bit too close to home."

We leave Charlie to his hay and the night and return to my friend's digs to do some more catching up, and in the morning I carry on with my trip. It's not until many months later I get around to ringing about Charlie.

"Yeah, he's good," the cameleer tells me.

"Ever find out who did it?"

"Nah. Been a bit of it about lately: animals hit with crossbows, kangaroos, sheep, but nothing around here. And Charlie's back to normal. Even bucked me off the other day."

"Well that's good: he's obviously feeling his oats."

"Yeah, I'm thinking of getting him castrated at the moment. Vet wants to charge me a thousand bucks so I reckon I'll do it myself."

Poor Charlie. Survived the crossbow to face the knife. Tough life for a camel.

MISSING THE ORIGINAL

To be honest I missed my opportunities this week. Drove from Broome to Carnarvon and failed to get a good story. I got fragments and whispers, promising leads that went cold in my hands, but nothing I thought I could turn into entertaining television.

I didn't do the camel story because I didn't think the story was strong enough without sensationalising, and I'd already featured camels earlier so I was reluctant to revisit the subject. In hindsight I may have been wrong on both counts. These days everyone loves a good bad behaviour story.

Last year when the mining boom was in full cry I heard there were boys sleeping in shipping containers, overturned water tanks, make-shift camps in the bush, anything, just to be near enough to get a piece of the action. The wages being paid by the mining companies were obscene and a kid fresh out of school could pull down 80K plus for driving a truck. So I called in to Port Hedland to do an alternative accommodation story but I was too late: things had gone off the boil. The Global Financial Crisis had seen China's demand for our iron ore drop and many a would-be miner was now waiting tables back in Perth.

Some good-natured coppers from Pannawonica pulled me over to recommend I visit Coral Bay – okay, I admit that wasn't their initial reason – so I obliged, and found a pretty coastal retreat where the most original thing I heard was, "Welcome to paradise and have a great day."

What constitutes a good story isn't always easy to define and is no doubt different for everyone, but I'm certain originality is at the core: be it a deed, a twist, or (especially) a person. I've resisted using the word "character" here because there isn't a soul breathing air that someone doesn't think is a character. Everyone's best friend is a character. Yet everyone's best friend is not an original in the sense I mean.

The fisherman in the picture* is an original. He doesn't need an introduction. He doesn't need his mates telling you he's a "character". It's plain to see the man does his own thing, thinks his own ideas.

I met him at Quobba fishing with his boys. It was late afternoon and they'd been fishing all day without success. I brought Mother Theresa alongside their 4x4 and got out. He spilled out of his rig with a fair degree of poise, and he looked exactly as you see him in the photo except he was holding a can of beer instead of a fishing rod. Even the smile was the same.

"How are you, mate?" I asked.

"Yeah, pretty pissed." It had been a very slow day on the rocks.

That night over a few more beers he agreed to let me video him fishing the next day.

"As long as you're not expecting me to be wearing all the flash gear."

"Wear what you're wearing now for all I care."

Which, of course, he did, was always going to do. In fact that's all I saw him wear the whole time: hat, briefs, thongs, smile.

* See photo, colour section one, page 4, top left.

Strictly speaking he's not a good advertisement for rock fishing – and yes I know it's Australia's most dangerous sport as I'm sure he does – but he's not trying to be an advertisement for anything. He's just being himself, an original.

He even used his spinning reel upside-down and back-to-front.

If I'd been smart I'd have hung a radio microphone around his neck and just shot the breeze while he was fishing. He'd have probably given me all the originality I needed. But I wasn't smart. I was too busy looking to see.

And in Carnarvon when I finally did come across the makings of a story I was so close to deadline I rushed it and didn't do it justice.

A ten-pound Pommy had built himself an electric car, which in itself wasn't ground breaking news, but he was such a good sport he could have kept you amused showing off a new toothbrush.

"I bought the old Camry from a bloke at Quobba for five hundred bucks," he began.

"He saw you coming."

"Yeah, didn't even make it home." He laughs, infecting the whole interview. He's got that mad professor look about him, and you can well imagine how a minor detail like whether the car worked or not would have escaped his attention.

He tells me he did most of the auto-electrical work involved in the conversion – though in that understated way the English have of telling you they just climbed Mt Everest but it was really no big deal, old boy, you could have done the same yourself – and when he takes me for a spin I'm surprised at how much torque it has.

"It'll sit you back in your seat like a formula one racing car," he laughs at his own exaggeration. In fact he never misses a chance to laugh at the silliness of it all.

"Because it runs silently I have to install an audio system to make it sound like a normal car, so people can hear me coming. Isn't that marvellous?

"And I've got an eighty-five-year-old engineer coming up from Perth to certify it roadworthy. Yeah, he's bringing his girlfriend with him," he says, smiling to himself.

"He's a proper engineer!" he qualifies, lest I be thinking the guy was a shonk. "Don't know if he knows anything about cars, but he's a real engineer."

And I wanted to stay and talk to him about his life as plantation owner in New Guinea and a farm manager in South Africa and any number of other interesting life adventures he'd had, but time was against me. And in the end I cut a story that was neither hand nor foot and wasted another original.

MUM'S THE WORD

Somewhere in the blur that was Western Australia in two weeks I believe I met the mother of a superstar. She was living in a small town in such an inconspicuous fashion that very few of its residents knew of her claim to international fame.

I learned of it picking some local's brains for story leads, and then only after I'd given up hope of finding anything worth pursuing. Then a man who'd listened quietly to my attempts at explaining the differences between obvious and interesting, mundane and quirky, offered a beauty.

"I can't guarantee she'll talk to you," he said, "and I'm not sure if this is the sort of thing you're after, but I know the mother of one of the boys from Abba lives here."

Not surprisingly, that set off such scoffing and challenging at the table that it was some time before I could bring the storyteller back to the point.

But eventually I learned he'd done some work for the old lady at some point and while he was there she'd told him – apropos of what I didn't establish, though I expect it could have been anything from an idle boast to an appropriate response to a simple question – that her son was a global superstar.

So I asked him if the old lady was "with faculty" as they say, because it's not uncommon for such ideas to sneak through the unprotected defences of a dementia-sufferer, but he assured me she was as lucid as a diamond.

Nobody else at the table knew of this woman's lustrous background and they weren't all accepting it now, but something about the off-hand way my storyteller delivered the news made me sense there was substance to it.

He was a tradesman and it was entirely plausible his work could have put him in a position to be having such a conversation with an old lady. Her age, too, was in the right ballpark. And that the mother of someone so famous might have sought to live in another country to escape attention – if that was her reason – also made perfect sense.

The fact that she'd managed to keep her identity almost completely to herself only made the story more intriguing, and for me was at the heart of the matter. That she was the mother of an internationally recognised performer gave her story the initial gloss, the gossip value, certainly, but how she ended up living in semi-reclusion in that particular town I found fascinating.

It's said if you want to hide you go to the city. To conceal anything in a country town requires a level of discipline usually reserved for professional criminals and obsessive compulsives. Since I could reasonably assume she was neither it made her story pretty special, so I encouraged my source to make contact on my behalf and request an interview.

As it happened my source went to ground the next day and I was forced to make my own enquiries, and the more I discovered people had no idea about the pop royalty living in their midst the more intrigued I became.

Eventually, using the scant details I had and the help of several independent sources, I tracked down a woman I believed to be the right one. She was living alone in a small unit in the centre of town and she came to the door promptly when I knocked.

She was a well-dressed woman with a small frame and fine facial features. Her eyes were bright and questioning.

I told her who I was and what I was doing and said I'd like to hear her story. When she asked why I said I'd heard she had an interesting history with links to a well-known rock group, though why I didn't just say who I thought she was I've no idea.

"No, not me," she said without the slightest trace of an accent. "Nothing to do with a rock group."

She neither scowled nor smiled when she said this but she spoke with such finality I felt it would be intrusive to push the point.

"Then I'm sorry for troubling you."

"Not at all," she said, her face still impassive.

And I left.

But something told me she was the woman I thought she was so I went back to the van and signed a copy of *Through Urban Eyes* for her, slipped in a business card and returned.

Again she answered the door without delay and again offered me the poker face.

"I thought you might like this book to read."

"Why?"

"Just my way of saying sorry to trouble you."

"Thank you. I like reading."

"Just one question."

"Yes?"

"Would your answer have been any different if I'd said pop group instead of rock group?"

"No," she shook her head, still no sign of a smile.

"Well, you'll find my card in there in case you do think of something you'd like to tell me."

Then she made her one and only slip.

"How did you find out?" she asked, before quickly re-phrasing the question to, "Where did you get the idea from?"

"People talk," I said. "As I'm sure you know."

"Well I hope you find who you're looking for."

"Thank you. And don't forget you've got my card if you need it."

Then she nodded and gave me a half smile. The dance was over.

And perhaps a smarter operator with a stealthier approach would have done better than me, but I suspect a woman who's concealed such a history from all but a few of her fellow residents in a quiet, country town would be more than a match for most.

And who knows? Maybe one day she'll want to tell her story and ring me, though I haven't heard from her yet.

NULLARBOR LOVING

Crossing the Nullarbor Plain for *Through Urban Eyes* I was at my lowest ebb for the trip, as flat as the land and running on empty. Then the country was brown and barren and felt like a mountain to climb, despite the obvious suggesting otherwise. This time everything was different. This time the Nullarbor was green. This time the Nullarbor produced and the long drive was over too soon.

Again I crossed west to east, using the Kalgoorlie Golf Course as my starting point. It was a Saturday afternoon but there was no sign of life. At the nearby bowls club I asked if anyone knew anything about the Nullarbor Golf project and got a cool reception.

"Any idea why there's nobody at the golf club on a Saturday afternoon?'

"Because it's not worth playing any day of the week."

Right. Obviously no love lost there. I didn't stay for an end.

The Nullarbor crossing is not what the first-time traveller might think. To begin with it's not all treeless plain as the name suggests; there's no shortage of timber for most of the way – Salmon Gums standing pink and proud amongst the copper-coloured mallee trunks, glorious yellow-barked eucalypts, even the mulga and the Spinifex have their own familiar charm – and along the relatively short stretch where nothing stands above a metre as far as the eye can see there's an eerie wonder to the experience, like driving on a vast, green (or brown) sea. The ocean, too, is a lot closer than you might imagine, and at certain times of the year you can view whales passing quite close to the sheered and jagged coastline. And there's a modest mountain pass to break the topography for an hour or two with its long time coming and going. So although the changes don't exactly dazzle, there is variety.

There's also a gusting, southerly wind blowing much of the time to keep a weary driver alert. For there's nothing like having your vehicle suddenly buffeted off the road to keep you on your toes.

Then there are the roadhouses with names like Mundrabilla, Cocklebiddy and Nundroo spaced out at semi-regular intervals along the way. If the Eyre Highway is the lifeline of the Nullarbor the roadhouses are its pulse, and how much you enjoy your trip will be greatly influenced by each stop you take. And if you dare linger at any of the roadhouses or small townships you'll likely discover things you never knew existed.

On this trip I tracked down the vineyard I mentioned in *Through Urban Eyes*, owned by an American who's either a visionary or a nutter, you take your pick, but he thinks we're mad for not realising the potential of the place and has ten acres under grape with more in the pipeline. There was no-one around when I arrived unannounced so I took some pictures of his set-up – a few sheds and water tanks, a big turkey's nest (dam), and the young Cabernet vines looking impossibly green against the muted greens and browns of the natural landscape – and then left. I'm told he intends to produce for the American market alone, but I hope he leaves a bottle or two for the sceptics back here. I know a lot of people would be interested to see what the Nullarbor produces.

I was also taken on a worthwhile detour to the coast at Penong and saw fully-grown Osprey chicks about to leave the nest and some little known and very beautiful coastal scenery. I was told the fishing was still spectacular thereabouts and the surfing even more-so, but the location was so jealously guarded that if I'd made the mistake of driving the heavily branded Mother Theresa in I'd have likely been driven out by a hail of rocks.

And along the way I met roadhouse operators full of fun and travellers full of awe and enjoyed every one of the thirteen hundred kilometres, shooting a good story about the golf links along the way (which should, by the time of publication, be another feature of the crossing). I arrived in Ceduna feeling good, as though the Nullarbor didn't get the better of me this time.

And it must have shown because no sooner had I settled in to edit my story than I was offered an indecent proposal. By a married man, if you don't mind.

Here's how it went.

First he knocked politely on the door while I was editing so I invited him in for a drink. I'd already met him when I first arrived and decided he was okay; a little effeminate, perhaps, but nothing to ring any alarm bells. It's rarely the first possibility I consider when I'm on the road: whether or not a man's going to hit on me, let alone one whose wife is sitting in their campervan twenty metres away.

Anyway, I quite liked him. He was friendly and not as obsessed with the price of petrol or how many experiences he'd ticked off his "bucket list" as a lot of caravan parkers seem to be. And when he finished his wine I refilled his glass and invited him around behind me to witness the "miracle" of laptop editing. In hindsight

I guess he could have taken these gestures as invitation to make a move, but I was still surprised when he put his hand on my shoulder ever so gently, ever so unnecessarily, and I realised he wasn't there for the creative process.

Now, I've had a bit to do with gay men over the years and usually found them good company, and I can't remember ever being offended by their occasional (and usually good-natured) advances. But there was something about this one I didn't like. Maybe it was the confined space, or maybe I just didn't like the stubbled beard and gold neck chain look of him, reminding me of someone who wasn't sure whether he wanted to be rock star or coal miner, so as soon as I sensed his hand settling in I swivelled around and shrugged it off, and he had no choice but to return to his seat across the table. I'm sure all women are familiar with this manoeuvre.

Then I waited for him to speak but he didn't seem inclined, as if I might not have noticed the slithering advances of a six-foot-two-inch paramour in my campervan. I didn't feel exactly threatened, but it did feel weird enough for me to imagine this must be close to what women mean when they speak of feeling physically intimidated by unwanted advances. I gave him a hard smile and held it.

"What?" he said, a portrait of innocence. He was smirking, wanting me to make the running. Because I didn't care for the elephant in the corner I did.

"Okay," I said. "The answer is no."

"What was the question?"

I put on a mask and shook my head.

"All right," he said after a long pause. "At this stage of my life I like to consider myself bi-sexual. My wife's not a very affectionate woman. Can you blame a man for trying?"

"No, I don't blame you," I said, thinking how inappropriate the old cliché "you're only human" really is at a time like this. Then I listened as he talked about his wife's psychiatric problems and how he cared for her thanklessly on the road, grateful we now seemed to be on safe ground.

But he had one more shot to fire.

"I have had success in these parks before, you know."

"Good for you."

He nodded and smiled, no sign of dented confidence now. "Last week there was a married man, a very macho married man, I might add. He was coy at first, too."

I showed him the palm of my hand. "I'm not interested, Brother."

"That's what he said."

"What's you wife's name?"

"Why?"

"Because in a second when I yell, 'Help! Your husband's got his willy out again.' I want to make sure I get the right wife. Apparently there's a lot of it about these days."

He gulped the last of his wine and looked at me, smiling. I smiled back, but this time I didn't refill his glass and the gesture was obvious. When he stood to leave he sighed long and hard.

"I guess I came here hoping you were bi-sexual, too."

I said nothing.

"But you're not."

"Correct."

He looked at me sadly and I felt a little sorry for him. But not sorry enough to say or do anything to encourage him. He turned and left.

I saw him again the next morning and we exchanged pleasantries as if nothing had happened. I wondered if his wife knew what he got up to while she was hiding in the darkness of their campervan, or if she was well enough to care. And I thought about the other grey nomads who needed more than sightseeing to keep them entertained, and how many would be surprised to learn that nothing ever changes, not even on the road.

In the end I decided it didn't bear thinking about but I still left Ceduna feeling a little flattened. Seems the Nullabor took its toll after all.

GOOD GRASS

Grass is a big thing on the Yorke Peninsula. In fact it's a big thing almost anywhere in dry old South Australia but they worship it on the yellow leg (check the map, you'll see the shape; and the yellow comes courtesy of the grain harvest).

The photo* was taken in Moonta, which forms part what they refer to as the Copper Triangle; Wallaroo and Kadina make up the

* See photo, colour section two, page 2, top.

other two co-ordinates. The region used to produce a wealth of copper, and at one point Moonta was the most populated town in South Australia, outside Adelaide. Maybe that's why they feel they still need the little trappings of urbanisation, like lawn.

You can see the owners have gone to some pains over this one. It may only be one little square but it's a beautiful green. Where the red topsoil came from I couldn't establish but it was obviously imported. It's freshly mown. And it's alive, the real deal.

The home's tenants told me they were unsure exactly how to care for the grass when they moved in so they contacted the owners.

"He told me to keep it short and it would stay green," the tenant relayed as if he was talking about some rare and exotic creature, which, of course, he was. "It was so long we've had to mow it a couple of times to get it down.

"We're only allowed a drip system here so we give it fifteen minutes a day."

I told him it looked fantastic and his face glazed over like mothers' do when you tell them their babies are beautiful.

As I continued down the street I saw other homes with well-kept gardens, as neat and creative as anywhere in the country, but always small, thoughtful affairs, and often with that little dash of green sometimes not much bigger than a floor mat.

It's so revered in these parts it's even used as a feature in real estate and holiday letting advertisements. To be able to mention your property has a patch of lawn is almost on par with having sea views.

Our obsession with lawn even pre-dates the invention of the lawn mower in the 1800s, and harks back to the Tudor and Elizabethan eras when it was the name given to a pasture kept short through constant grazing by livestock and rabbits. Then, only wealthy households could afford to keep a lawn tended by shearing and scything, and it really wasn't until the Jacobean period in the 1600s that the short-cropped English lawn became a bona fide status symbol.

Now it's a must-have for every house-proud urbanite from one green corner of the globe to the other.

According to a recent NASA sponsored survey, lawn is America's largest irrigated crop, covering almost 32 million acres. Keeping so much grass cut down to size was becoming such an issue, that in 1997 the Environmental Protection Authority mandated emissions control on new lawn mowers to reduce the summer smog.

In Canada, lawn pesticides are the main concern, and over 130 municipalities plus the entire province of Quebec prohibit the use of them.

And in Moonta, South Australia, it's getting enough water to grow a lawn that's the problem. The semi-arid climate may be just the business for barley, but keeping a lawn green in a 400ml annual rainfall belt can't be easy.

For the scientific community the main issue with lawn is the very real threat to biodiversity it poses, and at least one smart young thinker I know sees our pre-occupation with it as yet another example of our loss of touch with nature. I'm inclined to agree. It makes no sense, especially in this country, to persevere with such an environmentally unfriendly custom just to keep up with the Jones's, but persevere we do.

I even saw a bloke on the side of the road dealing the stuff out of the back of his ute. He had some samples spread out on the ground and two people looking interested so I stopped. I was amazed at how lush and green his product looked as I approached.

But as I neared I realised something was amiss: it was fake. He was peddling synthetic grass on the streets for up to seventy bucks a square metre laid. In broad daylight! I asked him how business was going.

"If it grows any faster it'll kill me," he said about that which sold itself on the very fact that it never grew, never died. "People get sick of looking at bare dirt all the time so they call me."

His clients were replacing the tiny patch of synthetic lawn they already had, which had faded in the sun. Just like giving real grass a dose of fertiliser, I guess. And just like real grass it came in a variety of colours and flavours. You could have light green, dark green, variegated (both together), or even the triple weave option which required no infilling with sand.

The couple were leaning towards the variegated because they liked the authentic look, and it certainly looked real enough, especially with the sand infill optional extra. I had to admire the ingenuity of the marketing people to come up with an add-on that would doubtless be added naturally over time anyway. Down the road at Port Hughes, work on the Greg Norman-designed golf links, The Dunes, had been suspended because of the airborne dust problem. Here they were flogging it out of the back of a truck. (Okay, that's a mild exaggeration, but you get my point.) I guessed it was only a matter of time before they started selling lawn mowers without blades and sprinklers that twinkled in the sun without using a drop of water.

That evening I got an email from the tenant wanting to know if his grass was going to be on television.

Almost, my friend, almost.

BUSH PILOT

I'd heard they had rain out Oodnadatta way so I rang a pilot I knew from William Creek to ask if there was water flowing into Lake Eyre. There was, he said, and of course he'd take me for a look. I knew there'd be a story in it but what shape it'd take I had no idea.

He picked me up from the airport they use to service the Olympic Dam mine site and flew me north. On the way we stopped to drop mail off to the stations along the way. When the roads are cut he becomes the mailman for this small community.

"Just doing a favour for the postie at Coober Pedy," he tells me.

Not to mention the station owners. He also delivers bread and milk and other essentials when required. Not surprisingly they fete him in these parts, with tea and biscuits, with praise, with gratitude.

Pretty soon it became clear that was my story – the flying mailman – Lake Eyre was just a bonus.

The dry red land of the year before was now covered in puddles, even great sheets of water in parts. Formerly barren rivers were now kilometres wide, sections of the train track were barely visible above the water and much of the road was under it. Everywhere the country had lost that parched, baked look as the soil soaked up the moisture.

"Best Christmas present we ever had," one station owner tells me over tea served with no fewer than four types biscuits made by his wife. It's marginal country out here and the dry spell had seen the stations all de-stock to absolute minimum levels; now they could re-stock.

The ritual is repeated at Anna Creek Station, a property bigger than Belgium in size: we drop the mail and exchange news over a cuppa and a biscuit. I'm beginning to see why the old parish priest was always in such healthy condition.

At the pink roadhouse at Oodnadatta the importance of these visits is summed up.

"We've run out of potatoes and onions," one of the proprietors tells me, "but we're not starving and the sun's shining, and Trevor kindly brought the mail for us.

"People say they couldn't live in the bush anyway without the Royal Flying Doctor Service," she adds. "Well I wouldn't like to live out here without Trevor."

But the man himself doesn't make a big deal of it. "It's only a small community and we've got to look after one another," he tells me later. I imagine the fuel costs alone would prevent most of us being so civic-minded.

True to form he takes a detour over Lake Eyre North on the way home, for my benefit. The water flowing in at the top end makes a shiny delta in the light of the setting sun, fanning out into an immense, shimmering arc over the salt bed of the lake. There hasn't been enough rain to fill the lake, not by a long stretch, but it's a rare and beautiful sight nonetheless.*

The surrounding landscape is rich red with a mottling of green and reminds me of photos I've seen of the surface of the moon, with chains of craters and fissures forming strange patterns in the soil. The flowers have just begun to bloom and I imagine it would be a delight to see at ground level in a month's time. We fly home in silence, savouring the experience.

"Only a handful of people have ever seen what you saw today," Trevor assures me later. "Australia's very lucky to have these river systems up here, untouched by man, still behaving as they always did."

He owns two of the three houses in William Creek and survives by taking tourists on scenic flights over the Painted Hills and Lake Eyre, and the odd charter for the mines. He keeps a tab over the bar at the pub and insists on buying my drinks, and feeds and accommodates me overnight.

Over a few beers he tells me he owns several planes and has difficulty keeping good pilots, with most moving on once they've learned the lessons only remote area flying can teach.

"Helps them read the conditions and think for themselves," he says. "They leave here much better pilots than when they came."

The couple running the pub seem close to the end of their tether. They're ready to sell up but the economic downturn has left them

* See photo, colour section one, page 1, bottom.

holding the baby, like so many others. If the lake fills with more rain it will be a good tourist season and they might be able to sell on the back of that, meantime they're left trying to eke a living out of five cars a day.

In contrast you get the feeling Trevor will survive any downturn. And he's about as benevolent as they come. He believes in the tourism potential of the area and that keeps him passionate. He maintains his planes well and trains young pilots as they come through. He drinks an occasional beer at the pub to stay in touch with his neighbours and entertains the media on request. And he does the mail run when it rains.

You wouldn't bite him even if you were a dog.

Footnote: when I returned six months later William Creek was a boomtown. Lake Eyre had water and Trevor was running about a dozen planes and still not keeping up with demand. The pub was humming and the proprietors now seemed close to the other end of their tether – the one reached through exhaustion – but at least they were smiling. Even the humble caravan park across the road was full of campers waiting to get on a scenic flight. Lake Eyre: she may be fickle, but when she turns it on all is forgiven.

THE WANDERERS

Driving through country New South Wales I come across an old green Kombi van so outrageously festooned it looks straight out of a children's adventure cartoon. The first thing I notice coming up from behind is the garden on the roof, complete with living flowers and herbs. Then I see the chimney poking into the sky, the wood panelling along the sides and the bay window protruding from the back. Lastly come the details: the decorative curlicues and arabesques, shiny things hanging from the side mirrors and a mysterious wooden box top-left; it seems the more I look the more it reveals.

I have no option but to make a citizens' arrest and pull the van over.

The driver is a busty hippy who isn't the least bit fazed by having a stranger flag her down. Indeed she immediately begins telling me how she normally rejects requests by the media to tell her story because she travels alone and doesn't want to advertise that fact, but this may be my lucky day because she's just recently found herself a travelling companion.

At this point she opens up the back of the Kombi to reveal a tallish man being held captive by a large rubber ball, or so it seems at first glance. In reality there just isn't a lot of space for a large man and ball alongside the wood burning stove, fridge, double bed, cupboards and whatever else is crammed into the thing.

I hadn't stopped smiling since I set eyes on the van and now I'm laughing. It's clear this is something special. But would she talk to me? Yes, but first she has to drop her dog off (yes, she even has a dog in there as well) to her son in the next town, to look after while she goes up to the Woodford Folk Festival.

"My predecessors were nomads who travelled from one energy field to the next," she tells me as she prepares us all French toast on the fuel stove. "Now I travel around helping people."

Okay, so she's a space cadet, but she has a warm smile and a nurturing way so it's not hard to imagine her playing Mother Carer.

"My son says I attract crazy people, but I tell him they're the ones who need the most help." I consider this remark for a moment but decide it's not directed at me: I'm a professional, after all.

Bacon is sizzling on the stove and she's beating eggs for the batter. A bottle of cream spills on the floor and she calls the dog in to lick it up. It's cosy with her, the dog, the camera and me all inside the van together.

She maintains a line of patter as she works and tells me how she has occasional troubles with councils moving her on, not allowing her to sleep in her "home" on the side of the road, but most places make her welcome. And she survives on donations and what business she can generate as a healer at markets and festivals.

Then she stops mid-sentence and startles me by climbing out of the van over the front seat, calling for her partner. For a moment I think I may have accidentally put my hand somewhere it wasn't invited, but it turns out she's seen a spider. She may be good with all things spiritual but the creepy crawlies make her blood run cold.

"Last week we had little grey fairies in the van," she tells me without explanation, "and I had to push an old lady out of the way to escape. But my man saved me, didn't you sweetheart?"

Her man mumbles something about "his duty" as he deals with the spider, which he's instructed to remove without harming. It takes me a while to work out the "fairies" she was referring to were mice.

But the star attraction of this outfit is definitely the Kombi. Several times while I'm talking to her people come to have a look at this curious vehicle. I ask one woman what she likes about it.

"Everything!" she says, with some enthusiasm. "Look, it's got a garden, a chimney, the smell of coffee wafting through. I want one."

"Happens all the time," the hippy tells me. "Even while we're asleep in the back people mill around, taking photos; I haven't the heart to open up the curtains and go 'Boo!'"

Then she shows me the little wooden box that caught my eye earlier. It's a Jack-in-the-box with a dragon instead of a Jack.

"Sometimes people get nosy while we're away from the van and they open up the box." She does so and the little rubber dragon springs out of the box. "It's supposed to have business cards attached to it, but I don't want people chasing me all over the place. If they really need me they can find me."

I agree it's not like she's hard to spot.

Easier to miss but no less unique is John*. He's walked the roads for thirty-odd years, the first twenty of those as a missing person. He set off as a young man with the intention of hitchhiking around

*See photo, colour section one, page 4, bottom left.

Australia between jobs. After a while he stopped sticking his thumb out and just walked. I found him just north of Tamworth.

"They call me the highwayman, the last swaggie, but they're just labels," he says.

He carries all he owns in a backpack, hessian shoulder bag and bed roll and admits to being a hoarder in spite of the limitations. "I have a cleanout every eighteen months or so," he tells me with a wry smile.

"A garage sale?"

"Nah, I just throw it in the bin. It's not worth anything, Just plastic sheeting and things I pick up along the road."

He survives by what he picks up on the roadside: a few coins, food scraps, the generosity of passing motorists. I give him a few fresh-baked scones and some fruit but he tells me to keep the apples because his can't eat them. Most of his teeth are rotted away to the gums but he hasn't seen a doctor in thirty years.

He sleeps in the bush at the side of the road and lights no fires.

"I've seen too many bushfires. I'd always be worried I didn't put my fire out properly. Besides, it's another thing to feed, to look after."

He's a slightly built man with ginger-white stubble and freckled, sunburnt skin. He wears a newish broad-rimmed felt hat someone gave him in Queensland, tinted glasses and grubby khakis that don't smell offensive. (Either that or I smelled worse than he.) He walks slowly, methodically in soft walking shoes and takes in the sights around him as the cars rush by.

Since he's been re-united with his family he writes a monthly letter to his mum. I ask him how his writing is after so long out of practice and he admits the grammar may not be perfect but he can still manage. "I'm a reader," he explains.

He tells me he's learned to read whatever he finds on the side of the road so I give him a copy of *Through Urban Eyes* since it probably qualifies as roadside fiction.

"How much have you changed in the thirty years?"

"I've probably grown into myself a lot more, learned to take everything as it comes, one foot in front of the other."

"Do you think it's a simple thing, this life?"

"Mine is," he replies.

My last and favourite wanderer I find hitchhiking on the outskirts of Rockhampton in Queensland. He looks the worse for wear and has a dog at his feet, so I pick him up because I figure it's unlikely anyone else will. When he gets in I see he has a fat lip with blood congealed around the edges. He tells me he got belted the day before.

"Yeah, some guy just lined me up. Didn't like me. Broke a couple of teeth. Look."

He opens his mouth to show me the damage and I wish I hadn't looked. There are teeth everywhere and he's having trouble talking. But he's a decent soul who considers having a chat about his life and times fair exchange for the lift, so he soldiers on.

He's Croatian-born and came here as a kid in 1968. His mother was a chronic depressive who eventually committed suicide by drowning herself in the Yarra. His father re-married and took his new wife back to Croatia. He has two sisters left in Australia who he doesn't see anymore and he doesn't know his nieces and nephews. His most recent job was mining for opal in Coober Pedy, but from what I can gather that was some time ago, and these days he collects the pension and travels the country as a free camper.

His companion is a fat red cattle dog called Zucho, which is as close as I can get to the spelling of the Croatian word for his colour. When he boards he does a lap of the bus to check it out then sits protectively between us up the front.

"I rescued him from Coober Pedy," his master tells me. "He was just a skinny runt, then."

When the dog plonks his body down his haunches shake like jelly in the aftershock; if the skinny runt is still in there somewhere he's getting a cushioned ride. Zucho tolerates me giving him a pat, but when I reach towards my passenger to point out something on the road map he pushes my hand away with his snout, making sure I don't get too friendly with his food source.

As we drive the hitchhiker tells me how Rockhampton hasn't treated him too well.

"Yesterday morning I woke up in the park and someone had stolen my knapsack. All I had left were the clothes I'm wearing and my blanket.

"By lunchtime it was really hot so I took Zucho for a swim in the lake. When I got back to the BBQ where I'd thrown my jacket it had burnt a big hole in the back of it. Someone had cleaned the hotplates and forgotten to turn them off.

"So I decided to go the pub to change my luck and that's when the bloke knocked my teeth out."

"So then I came back to the park and kept drinking to ease

the pain, and by and by this girl walks past so I ask her if she wouldn't mind a bit."

"How could she resist?"

"Yeah," he grins through his busted mouth, "but somehow she held herself back and next thing I've got the cops locking me up for being a public nuisance.

"And when they let me out this morning I had to go and bail Zucho out of the pound."

Clearly he's had a big twenty-four hours and I'm not surprised when he starts nodding off in his seat.

"Sorry I'm not great company," he says. "Suddenly I feel very tired."

"Go right ahead, brother."

"Thanks," he says, and drops off to sleep in an instant. Ten minutes later he wakes with a start.

"What's this town you're dropping me off in?"

"Gin Gin. Then you've got about fifty kilometres to Bundaberg."

"Gin Gin," he says like he's trying out an exotic new word. "I've never been to Gin Gin. With a name like that they'd have to have a pub there, wouldn't they?"

"I guarantee it. In fact I daresay they'll have more than one."

"Good. I like having a beer in a new pub. It's one of my favourite things."

Then he gives the dog a scratch and goes back to sleep with a smile on his crooked face.

SAD FAREWELLS

I'm sorry to say Mother Theresa didn't make it. While I was driving around in limbo after the Sunrise sacking she died in my arms. Vehicles tend to do that on me. Like the baker on the Eyre Peninsula said when he saw the state of The Parrot* on the first trip, "Yeah, I'm usually the last owner a car ever has, too."

Maybe she went out in sympathy with me, or maybe I was too hard on her, I don't know. But that's academic now because she's dead, or was when I last saw her. Gearbox, I think, though I never got the full story. In the end I think Winnebago were just happy to get her back in one piece and out of my hands. I had girlfriends' families feel that way when I was younger.

So I needed a new rig, an unbreakable, Monte-proof affair. After two trips and as many broken vehicles it was time to set myself up with a more robust outfit.

Spurring me on was the signing of a contract with Australia Network to produce sixty Postcards as quickly as possible. AN is the digital broadcasting arm of ABC International – though financed by the Department of Foreign Affairs and Trade – and reaches over forty countries throughout the Asia-Pacific region. The Network was planning to use them as interstitials to fill the gaps between regular programming, and gave verbal indication that they'd take even more beyond the contracted number.

* The Hymer Happy Tramper I drove around the country collecting the stories that inspired the first of the **RED IN THE CENTRE** series: ***Through Urban Eyes***.

In addition to AN, Tourism Australia contracted me to produce some travelogues, so with two clients on board I had incentive enough to bite the bullet and go freelance.

My friends were doubtful.

"Do you really think it's wise for you to be investing your own money in a *campervan*?" came the common refrain, usually emphasizing the last word as if all I'd ever done in my life was kill the things. I was reminded of the old chestnut, Lucky Pierre, the all-conquering adventurer who had the incredible misfortune of being caught *in flagrante delicto* with a common farmyard animal, and was forevermore known only for that sordid little deed in spite of his many subsequent feats of courage and derring-do.

I assured them "wise" had very little to do with humanity's greatest endeavours, and besides, it was now necessary since I'd sold all my real estate and had nowhere else to live; unless, of course, they were offering a spare room at their house. That invariably shut them up.

Choosing an appropriate vehicle wasn't easy. I'd been to school on The Parrot and Mother Theresa, and while both had their merits I thought neither had the capability (or durability) to cover the terrain I wanted to access. I needed a 4x4 with enough space to live in and well-enough known to get service in the bush. I was surprised to learn how limited the options were.

There were several light truck 4x4 options that had merit, but I didn't like the idea of driving a truck around the country (or the city, for that matter) or having the camper body built into a container on the trayback (rather than have the camper and cab incorporated in the one body). And there were various 4x4 conversions I'd heard about, but that option would have taken time and money I didn't think I could afford, and I wasn't sure my sources were reliable anyway. But it seemed there was nothing in-between.

Then I stumbled across a fully imported Hino Liesse 4x4 diesel with 180K on the clock that seemed to answer all my needs.

For the uninitiated (as I was), a Hino Liesse is effectively a Toyota Coaster bus – the transport of choice for many clubs and community groups these days – since it's made in the same factory and simply badged differently on the way out. The factory 4x4 option is very rare in this country – most 4x4s you see are conversions – and I was hoping it would open up much of the central and northern parts of the country normally inaccessible to two-wheel-drive campervans. I also figured it would be easy enough to service being a stable mate of the commonest make in the bush, Toyota, and confidently assured one of my doubting mates that any bush mechanic would be able to fix it with an old Cruiser carcass, duct tape and fencing wire. "Yeah, right," he said.

For the hard-core it has a four cylinder 4.1ltr, inter-cooled turbo diesel motor, with most of the running gear, I was (unreliably) informed, interchangeable with a Toyota Dyna 4x4. (Turned out parts were sourced variously from Coaster, Cruiser, Dyna and something they drive only on Mars). I added an extra 100ltr fuel tank to the existing 80ltrs, plus a gas conversion with a capacity of 30ltrs (inadequate), giving me a potential range of well over a thousand kilometres in theory. (In reality the mix proved difficult to regulate and gas wasn't readily available in the bush anyway, so I'd give it a miss next time.) Then came the internal camper fit-out, water tanks, solar panels, battery banks, inverters, generator, air conditioner, water heater, security system, spare tyre racks and sundry add-ons and modifications too numerous to list.

Needless to say this all took time to organize – not to mention the rigmarole involved in selling my only child to finance the show – and during the initial stages I parked myself in Bondi again and concentrated on lining up the ducks in preparation.

There was new software to be mastered, a website to be updated, loud signage (even louder than The Parrot) to be developed and applied, houses to be sold and contact arrangements streamlined, and basically a hundred other details that needed attention in preparation for going freelance and becoming a career vagrant.

And while my life was carrying on its busy way someone else's ended. We called him Claude and I loved him like a brother. We met as psychiatric nurses when he was just emerging from his first marriage with a mighty lust for all he'd missed, and I was a wild young tear-away up for anything. He was nuts and I was crazy and we were, for a time, inseparable. Together we visited places of the heart and mind neither had seen before or since. And even as our common interests faded like the red from his hair and the stars from my eyes we stayed close. Saying goodbye was one of the hardest things I've ever done.

So when it came time to name the new rig the choice was easy. A partner for an adventure into the unknown could be called nothing but Claude.

TEETHING PROBLEMS

The late Claude always was a complicated character. Sometimes he was so quiet you forgot he was there. At others you couldn't shut him up. To say he was unpredictable was to wrongly assume there was order in the first place. He was a willful soul, without doubt, and from an early stage his namesake showed similar traits.

I finally took possession of the new Claude after many months of delays, and spent the last couple of days sleeping *in situ* in the workshop while the finishing touches were applied. We thought this would be the best way to test the fit-out before I hit the road. He didn't wait long to show his hand.

The first time I tried out the shower the bastard locked me in. It's a fancy unit with a retractable screen, but once I'd pulled it shut it stayed that way. I was nude, wet and trapped in my own campervan parked in a closed workshop on an industrial estate after five pm. I didn't yell for help: even if someone had heard me I couldn't imagine how I might be rescued with dignity. For tools I had a shaving razor and a plastic soap caddy. I thought about trying to squeeze out though the roof vent but the prospect of getting stuck and compounding my indignity raised too many questions: From which end would they mount the rescue? Did I really want anyone using power tools around my delicate ensemblery? Would they draw faces on my arse and take photos? Eventually I pulled the unit apart with my bare hands and escaped, shaken but clean. First points to Claude.

For his next trick he waited till I was two days out and he jettisoned the spare tyres from their brand new rack, just threw them off like they weren't even attached. I spent half a day backtracking to and fro over the same stretch of dirt road to find them and in the process left myself without enough diesel to get to the next town. I had to resort to begging some from a passing farmer like a dandy from the city. It's hard to justify that kind of oversight when you're driving a lurid red and blue bus with your own face grinning like a loon from every panel. And the improved consumption from the expensive gas conversion didn't help either, because a) the filling nozzle had already jammed; and b) there was no gas to be bought out there anyway.

Then I noticed serious oil coming from the front wheel hub, signaling the start of a long-running battle with bearings and seals and shims and what-have-you, and forcing me to learn more about a motor vehicle's inner workings than I ever wished to know. It also marked the dreadful discovery that replacement parts would take a month to arrive from Japan, thereby blowing my theory out the window that I could fix Claude anywhere with fencing wire and duct tape.

And I hadn't even made it from Brisbane to Birdsville!

In Birdsville I got lucky and found an excellent steel fixer to build me a new tyre rack. He was the son of one of the service station owners and between them they sorted out several problems and alerted me to a couple more – namely the cause of the oil leak and the nationality of the necessary replacement – so we ended up about even.

Just to the north of Birdsville I got one back on Claude. They were grading a stretch of road so wide and flat it could have been an airstrip. I stopped and had an enjoyable yarn with the lollipop man, as is my wont, then proceeded through. I kept well to the right of the grader as I passed and stayed there for a couple of hundred metres to spare him my dust. (Why I thought this was a necessary courtesy to extend to a man in an air-conditioned cabin I have no idea, but I guess I was feeling benevolent after getting lucky with the tyre rack.) Anyway, it was such a good road I soon found myself cruising along at a fair old clip, gazing over the countryside with the calm of a man who has everything in his life under control, only seeing the guidepost directly in my path after I noticed its mate on the other side of the road and wondered why on earth they'd put one of those in the middle of such a great piece of roadwork. Then I whacked mine dead centre and bent it over like a felled tree. And they're not plastic these days, either, but some sort of alloyed metal. I know because I went back to straighten it up: the road crew was still in sight and I didn't want the boys thinking I didn't care. When I came back through the same road plant the next day the lollipop man was in his truck and tooted his horn madly at me to stop, but I ignored him. I couldn't imagine the conversation being nearly so enjoyable two days running.

Claude and I made it down the Birdsville Track without further mishap, but before we'd gone far along the Oodnadatta Track I noticed the brakes getting a bit squeaky. My supplier had assured me he'd changed the pads so I put it down to dust infiltration – Christ knows it had infiltrated every one of my orifices it seemed plausible enough it would affect the externally housed brakes – and it wasn't until I overshot the Stuart highway at Marla that I realised how bad they were. Luckily there was no traffic in my path at the time and the shrubbery wasn't too substantial at my point of entry.

I'd also been having trouble keeping the tyre racks in place. The Birdsville-designed rack was a beauty, but they'd stayed with the original fasteners, which were useless. The catches were positioned too close to the pivots and a good bump would bend the metal and free the racks, so I'd be driving down the road unaware the two wheels were sticking out the back like Mickey Mouse ears. It was only drawn to my attention when I noticed other drivers taking their cars well off the road as I approached and not returning my wave of thanks. Afterwards it occurred to me they were probably too pre-occupied with staying alive out there.

Another thing I noticed as I made my way up the Stuart Highway was the absence of taillights. Whether this matter bore any relation to the Christmas tree of lights I now had on the dash I didn't know, I couldn't make head or tail of the icons. I only knew that if I applied the brakes my speed didn't diminish, the brake lights wouldn't come on and for all intents and purposes it was the same as if I did nothing. But if I drove slowly and kept one eye on the rear vision mirror there was a better than average chance I'd make it to Alice Springs without wiping anyone out with my Mickey Mouse ears.

It was an inglorious beginning.

But I'm getting ahead of myself. There are people to meet before I get to the Alice, and places to go. Claude is not the star of this show and I must not allow his selfish antics to upstage the whole cast. Let me take you back to Lake Eyre country.

PELICAN MAN

"I could have shot some remarkable vision last time I was here," the photographer tells me excitedly, "only I blew it. I'd just put the video camera on the ground when I saw with my own eyes a crow fly down and pick up a pelican chick small enough to fit in my hand. Then out of the pack comes a hero to the rescue: a half-grown juvenile appears and knocks the crow for six so it drops the chick. Then to my horror the juvenile pelican picks up the chick it just saved and eats it! Can you believe that, Monte? And that didn't happen just once, either, but twice I saw. And here I was thinking they were the gentle giants of the sky, and they're cannibals!"

For some reason the concept of cannibalism in the Australian Pelican ranks doesn't quite fit with our image of the bird. Yet if you do a quick search on the Internet you'll find ample video proof of pelicans eating live ducks and pigeons at the zoo, taken by shocked tourists and parents with some subsequent explaining to do. Not to mention quite a number of articles and references in scientific journals and papers about the behaviour. And now I can confidently add the look on my photographer's face as solid anecdotal evidence.

When I arrived at the rookery there wasn't a soul around save him and the pelicans. Though he'd already been there five days his camp was the most Spartan of affairs, with only his swag and a small gas stove sitting on the ground next to his 4x4, which was parked under the only shade tree in sight. A short distance away were the two empty foldaway chairs where we're now seated,

THE COLOURS

Above: *Random Salt Pan, SA* (story page 106).

Below: *Lake Eyre North, SA* (story page 79).

THE STATS

MOTHER THERESA

Vehicle:
Winnebago Birdsville on a Fiat Ducato 3ltr 2WD diesel

Distance:
Approx 35,000kms

Time:
4 months

Bogged or broken:
Once (story page 36)

Best feature:
The Luton Peak (overcabin bed/ storage area)

Worst feature:
The Luton Peak (kept hitting my head)

Summary:
Good entry-level camper for blacktop touring.

CLAUDE

Vehicle:
Fully imported Hino Liesse (aka Toyota Coaster) 4.1ltr 4WD diesel

Distance:
Approx. 25,000kms

Time:
5 months

Bogged or broken:
Give me a break! (stories throughout)

Best feature:
4WD capabilities

Worst feature:
Auto-electrics front and back

Summary:
Import equals headache for parts and service, but otherwise ideal for my purposes.

Map is representative only.

LEGEND	BY ROAD	BY AIR	BY SEA
Mother Teresa			
Claude			

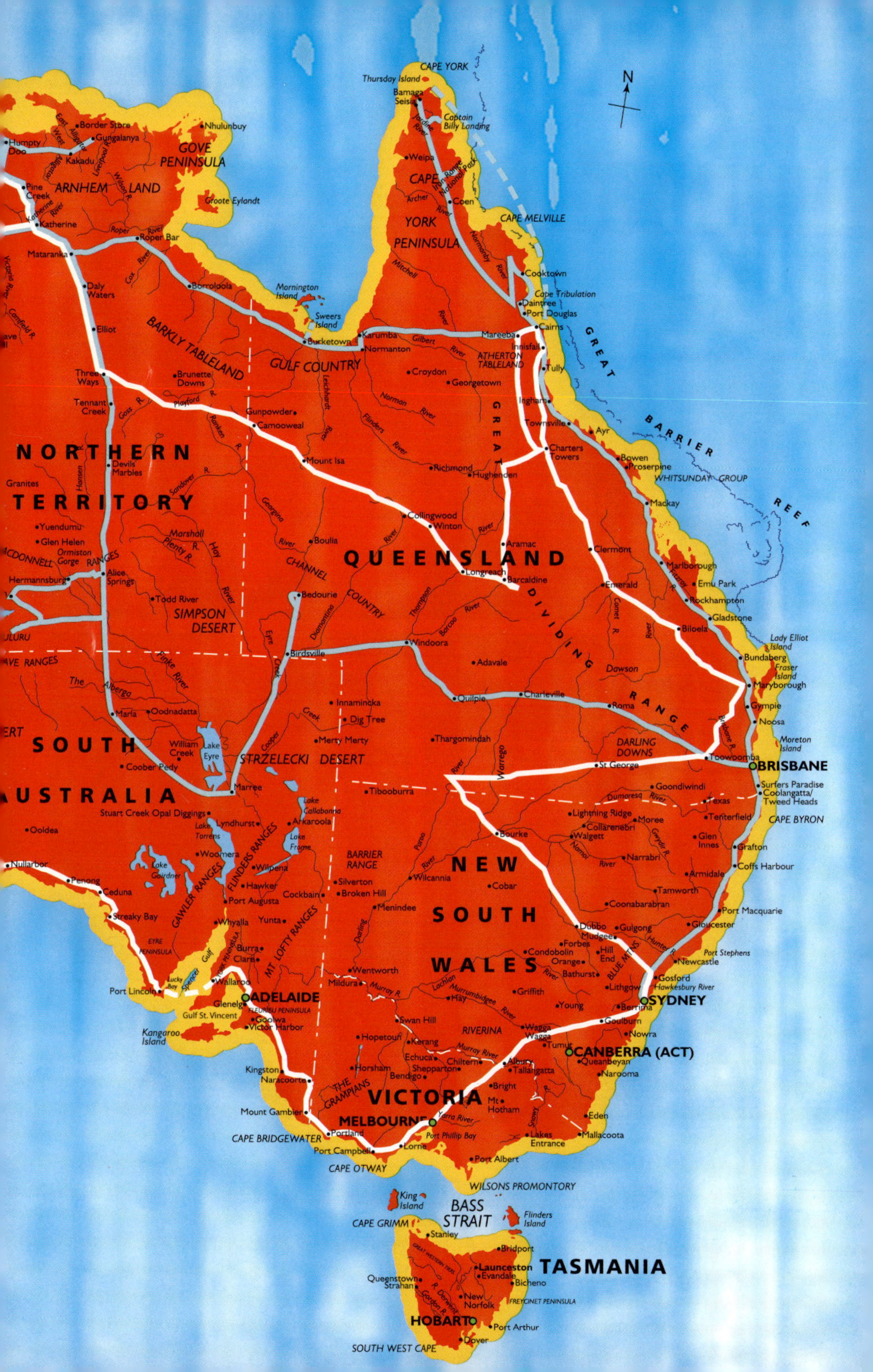

N
CAPE YORK
Thursday Island
Bamaga
Seisia
Captain Billy Landing
Weipa
CAPE YORK PENINSULA
Coen
CAPE MELVILLE
Cooktown
Cape Tribulation
Daintree
Port Douglas
Cairns
Mareeba
ATHERTON TABLELAND
Innisfail
Tully
Ingham
Townsville
Charters Towers
Ayr
Bowen
Proserpine
WHITSUNDAY GROUP
Mackay
GREAT BARRIER REEF
Nhulunbuy
GOVE PENINSULA
Border Store
Gungalanya
Humpty Doo
Kakadu
ARNHEM LAND
Groote Eylandt
Pine Creek
Katherine
Roper Bar
Mataranka
Daly Waters
Borroloola
Mornington Island
Sweers Island
Burketown
Karumba
Normanton
Elliot
BARKLY TABLELAND
GULF COUNTRY
Croydon
Georgetown
Three Ways
Brunette Downs
Tennant Creek
Gunpowder
Camooweal
Mount Isa
Richmond
Hughenden
NORTHERN TERRITORY
Devils Marbles
Granites
Yuendumu
Glen Helen
Ormiston Gorge
Hermannsburg
Alice Springs
Todd River
SIMPSON DESERT
Boulia
Collingwood
Winton
Aramac
QUEENSLAND
Longreach
Barcaldine
Clermont
Emerald
Marlborough
Emu Park
Rockhampton
Gladstone
Biloela
CHANNEL COUNTRY
Bedourie
GREAT DIVIDING RANGE
Birdsville
Windoora
Adavale
Lady Elliot Island
Bundaberg
Fraser Island
Maryborough
Gympie
Noosa
Quilpie
Charleville
Roma
Dawson
Innamincka
Dig Tree
Merty Merty
Thargomindah
DARLING DOWNS
Toowoomba
BRISBANE
Moreton Island
Marla
Oodnadatta
SOUTH AUSTRALIA
William Creek
Lake Eyre
Coober Pedy
STRZELECKI DESERT
St George
Goondiwindi
Surfers Paradise
Coolangatta/Tweed Heads
CAPE BYRON
Marree
Tibooburra
Stuart Creek Opal Diggings
Lyndhurst
Arkaroola
Lightning Ridge
Moree
Texas
Tenterfield
Ooldea
Lake Torrens
Lake Frome
Collarenebri
Walgett
Bourke
Glen Innes
Grafton
Woomera
Wilpena
FLINDERS RANGES
BARRIER RANGE
NEW SOUTH WALES
Narrabri
Coffs Harbour
Nullarbor
Penong
Ceduna
Lake Gairdner
GAWLER RANGES
Hawker
Port Augusta
Silverton
Broken Hill
Cockburn
Wilcannia
Cobar
Armidale
Tamworth
Coonabarabran
Port Macquarie
Streaky Bay
Whyalla
Yunta
Menindee
MT LOFTY RANGES
Dubbo
Gulgong
Mudgee
Gloucester
EYRE PENINSULA
Burra
Clare
Condobolin
Forbes
Orange
Hill End
Bathurst
BLUE MTNS
Port Stephens
Newcastle
Gosford
Hawkesbury River
Lithgow
Berrima
SYDNEY
Wentworth
Mildura
Port Lincoln
Wallaroo
ADELAIDE
Glenelg
Hay
Griffith
Young
Gulf St. Vincent
FLEURIEU PENINSULA
Goolwa
Victor Harbor
Swan Hill
Goulburn
Nowra
Kangaroo Island
Hopetoun
Kerang
RIVERINA
Wagga Wagga
Tumut
CANBERRA (ACT)
Queanbeyan
Narooma
Echuca
Shepparton
Chiltern
Albury
Tallangatta
Kingston
Horsham
Bendigo
Naracoorte
THE GRAMPIANS
VICTORIA
Bright
Mt Hotham
Mount Gambier
MELBOURNE
Yarra River
Eden
CAPE BRIDGEWATER
Portland
Port Phillip Bay
Lakes Entrance
Mallacoota
Port Campbell
Lorne
CAPE OTWAY
Port Albert
WILSONS PROMONTORY
King Island
BASS STRAIT
Flinders Island
CAPE GRIMM
Stanley
Bridport
Launceston
Evandale
TASMANIA
Bicheno
Queenstown
Strahan
New Norfolk
FREYCINET PENINSULA
HOBART
Port Arthur
Dover
SOUTH WEST CAPE

THE CHARACTERS

Top left: *An Original, Quobba, WA* (story page 61).

Top right: *Spanish Denial, NT* (story page 41).

Bottom left: *John the Walker, roadside, NSW* (story page 83).

Bottom right: *The Gentleman Cowboy, Gympie, QLD* (story page 34).

THE PEST & THE CONTROLLER

Above: *The Savvy Bugman, Mundubbera, QLD* (story page26).

Below: *Cane Toad on Casey's Dinner, Goat Island, NT* (story page 148).

THE BITIES

Above: *The New Guard, Wyndham, WA.*

Below: *Got Any Dogs? Aileron, NT* (story page 47).

THE ROADSIDE ATTRACTIONS

Above: *Anmatjere Woman & Child, Aileron, NT* (story page 45).

Below: *Barra Boasting, Cape York, QLD*.

THE COMMUNICATION TREE

The Savannah Way, Gulf Country NT.

facing the nearest of the birds. And that was it. Not even the remnants of a fire.

Nobody appeared when I first pulled up and I assumed he was out amongst the birds somewhere, so I unpacked my camera gear to shoot some vision while I waited for his return. But as I walked past his vehicle I saw a bent knee protruding from the open front door. He was sitting in the passenger seat working on his laptop, so absorbed in his work that he hadn't heard me drive in and park not thirty metres away.

He was wearing shorts, odd socks and no shoes because "life's not perfect". And although it was a warm afternoon he had his flannelette shirt buttoned to the neck. A backwards baseball cap added the finishing touch to "his uniform".

I wasn't sure what reception to expect; the owner of the property had told me the photographer was camped out here researching the pelicans alone, but he greeted me like an old friend and ushered me towards the deck chairs. I was only his third visitor this stretch (he'd already spent two weeks with the pelicans a month beforehand, when the cannibalism episode was played out), and one could easily imagine he was eager for company. Not so.

"People often ask me if I get lonely out here, but I'm too busy to get lonely.

"When my friends heard I was coming back to see the pelicans again they couldn't understand why. 'Aren't you over it yet?' they said. But how can you get over a sight like this?'

It was, indeed, an incredible sight. Occupying perhaps twenty acres of land around the lake were so many pelicans the estimates varied between thirty and fifty thousand birds, a range so broad you could hardly accept any one as gospel. They came to breed, and only did so when the Lake Eyre system was filled sufficiently to support the raising of chicks, conditions that occurred very rarely. For this was bull dust, sand and salt lake country, sparsely vegetated and normally incapable of sustaining life in numbers above single figures. Yet before me was an undeniable heave of life, a seething, squawking stench of adolescent feathers, gaping beaks and regurgitated fish matter, attended by harried parents performing their irresistible duty amongst the excrement and lice and carcasses of the fallen.

"Beautiful, isn't it?" Pelican Man brings me back to the here and now. "And the amazing thing is it's all over in three months. From the time the eggs hatch till the time the babies fly. Last time I was here there were chicks everywhere. Now they're almost fully-grown. It's unbelievable. And who knows if I'll ever get the chance to see this again."

He's a photographer who specializes in skyscapes, and he'd been working on a book on pelicans on the side when he heard about the breeding event. He tells me this is icing on the cake for that project, and as he speaks he never stops taking photographs and pointing out what I should be looking for.

"There's one feeding over there, see? See how the chick gets its beak right down the mother's throat till even its head disappears? Sometimes the parents have to thrash their heads from side to side to get them out when there's nothing more to regurgitate. Then the chicks just collapse on the ground like they're drunk. It's the stomach acid; so strong it makes them psycho."

From our vantage about twenty metres from the wall of birds we see the scene above played out many times. It's afternoon and the parents are returning from their day's fishing to feed the chicks. They come in squadrons of six or eight or more, sometimes flying in V-formation, breaking off on approach and scanning the crowd below before dropping in like stealth bombers right next to their own. It's an impressive performance that sends Pelican Man into raptures.

"Look at that!" he marvels. "And we can't find our own kids in a crowd at the football, even wearing different clothes."

He speaks with an engaging, boyish enthusiasm not easy to find in a man of his years – about fifty – and he's what's known in my industry as good talent.

I ask him how he thinks the birds know the breeding event is on and it becomes apparent he has strong religious beliefs. Not for him any scientific rationale. He's satisfied to know the big fella's got it all under control, and the whole show's been made possible by the instinct bestowed on all living creatures by God.

I'm not as convinced of its origins but I agree there's a collective instinct involved, though what triggers it I can't fathom. Most of these birds normally live a thousand or more kilometres away on the coast and only breed when conditions are suitable. Yet how can they know when sufficient rain has fallen in catchments sometimes a thousand kilometres distant form their breeding sites, to warrant taking the gamble?

Some believe it's simply a question of degrees, and that the birds make reconnaissance trips when inland rain falls, communicating their findings back to base. But remember these birds need to make their decision at least four months in advance, even before the magnitude of the flooding can be known – at least by humans, with all our wisdom – so there are some serious odds being played very well by the birds.

Occasionally they do get it wrong. Sometimes they start a colony somewhere on the system only to have to abandon their eggs unhatched when the water dries up prematurely. But most often when they make the effort they succeed in raising their young.

There are other wonders of Lake Eyre we *do* understand. Like how the fish suddenly appear as if fallen from the sky – they come with the floodwaters and their aggressive colonizing sometimes leaves them high and dry when the water recedes or evaporates. And how the Desert Frogs survive years, even decades between rains by burying themselves in water sacs in the mud. But for me the pelicans' story remains a mystery.

But Pelican Man doesn't waste energy on such conundrums. He's a passionate photographer with an understanding of the birds' behaviour you could only get by observing them for long periods of time, but he's no ornothologist. His interest is *naïve*, in the artistic sense of the word, and I accuse him of having fallen in love with the pelicans.

"Yeah, I do, I love them. It's an emotional time for me, leaving something like this. You wait till the morning when these babies are all out there in that lagoon learning how to fish, picking up sticks and stones and tossing them into the air and catching them with their beaks. Or when they all line up along the ridge there and flap their wings getting ready to fly, like a big school of the air for pelicans. It'll blow you away." And he bangs off three quick shots, as if to emphasize his point.

And his photographs show his passion. The colour and clarity he gets is astounding, and the compositions show, well, a love of his subject.

Over a campfire that night – when I first suggest one he scans the landscape littered with countless fire-sized sticks the pelicans use to decorate their nests with and asks, "Where will we get firewood?" – he tells me he's got plenty of good shots but he'll probably stay a couple of days more anyway. I don't realise why till the next morning, when he observes that it looks like some of the chicks have already flown.

"Do you think they all go together, or in dribs and drabs?" he asks wistfully.

That's when the penny drops: he's waiting for his babies to leave home. He wants the empty nest shot, as painful as it may be to witness.

Footnote: A week later I received an email from him saying he'd left the birds, but he was planning to return to "see if there's another stage to shoot". For more information on photographer Pete Dobre, visit www.petedobre.com

EYRE DINKUM

So you see a story on the television about Lake Eyre filling up and you throw the family in the car and set off to see the great lake full of water just once before you die. It's only happened half a dozen times in two hundred years, you tell the kids, and we may never get another chance. They say cool Dad.

But when you get there it's more like a bleak and salty moonscape than a lake and you can't see any nesting seabirds or wildflowers blooming for Christ's sake you can't even see any water and you've towed the boat a thousand kilometres for nothing and the kids say not cool Dad and your wife says many things besides.

Don't worry, you're not the first to make the trip for this result and you won't be the last.

In fact the great explorer Charles Sturt bashed around in the scrub for years and never even found it, so convinced was he that there was an inland sea out there somewhere, had to be because so many rivers ran that way, he reasoned, reasonably.

In 1840-41 Edward John Eyre did find the "inland sea" and was so unimpressed he called it "one vast, low, and dreary waste" and it was probably only thanks to a last minute rush of vanity that he allowed the authorities to give it his name.

Then explorers like Lewis, Warburton, Madigan and Halligan came and were variously disappointed and disparaging, the latter even trekking in with camels and boat after flying over the Lake and seeing it partly full, only to find it empty by the time he arrived with his exploration party four months later.

Of course these days visitors are more discerning and many enjoy, even prefer the stark beauty of the Lake without water. But there's no doubting the mystique surrounding a Lake Eyre with water, or the elusiveness that continues to taunt us two hundred years after white man first started wondering where all the water goes.

Yet to understand a Lake Eyre event you really need to look at the Basin as a whole – an area roughly a sixth the size of the continent, covering over a million square kilometres across three states and one territory – for it is always the contributing system that will hold the key to the highlights.

The media doesn't set out to mislead the public by showing images of life abounding in the desert – heaven forbid the media would ever sensationalise a story – but it does focus on the dynamic. Vision of fifty thousand nesting pelicans will always take precedence over images of a barren lake and a dour scientist talking the event down. And even if the pelican rookery is a thousand kilometres away from the lake, as far as the media's concerned it's one and the same story. And so it is.

In 2009 most of the water came from the Georgina system in western Queensland, which was collected by the Warburton for transport to Lake Eyre North. Logically, then, most of the juicy bits were along that system.

The main pelican rookery, for example, was north of Birdsville, many hundreds of kilometres upstream from the Lake. While I missed the best of the wildflowers as I travelled through that country I saw enough to imagine the showing would have been spectacular in pockets, especially where the floodwaters had come and gone. And one cattle property I visited had grass so good the station manager ate a handful to prove it to me.

"A bloke told me he once dropped a knitting needle in this grass," he said, "and came back two years later and found a crowbar."

Needless to say the cattle were fat. Some could barely raise a trot.

I saw the ruins of Annandale Station, one of Cattle King Sir Sydney Kidman's early acquisitions, and it was easy to grasp why he thought so highly of that country. The grass was as tall as a man in parts and thick beds of clover carpeted the finger plains between the rich, red sand hills. Kidman's theory was that if he owned enough land he could drought proof his stock by constantly moving them onto country with feed. By the time he finished he owned a string of properties covering over 3% of the country and no doubt many, many crowbars.

The original custodians also moved with the food, and you can still see evidence of the Wagkangurru people living out on the finger plains when the water brought life: a small jumble of rocks signifying the remnants of a campfire here, a larger, longer jumble marking a grave site there. I wouldn't have identified these myself, but my guide for the day was a Wagkangurru man who'd been raised by his grandparents. He remembered times of plenty, and also the cunning of his elders.

"In these parts you find kopi, gypsum I think you call it, and you see it in layers exposed on the sides of certain hills. Now, when there's a lot of moisture in the air the kopi sweats, and the elders knew this. So when conditions were right they'd make a point of hunting close to the kopi layers to keep an eye out for the sweating. And when they saw that happening they'd break off a piece of kopi and call the tribe together for a corroboree to dance for rain. More often than not it would rain and they were much revered for their rainmaking powers."

And there's a lot of common sense in this "sleight-of-hand" wisdom, just as there was in the locals using the Basin's rim as a trade route. Long before white man set foot there was a bustling exchange of tools and weapons, ochre and pituri, stories and songs between tribes thousands of kilometres distant. By following the natural springs and watercourse they were able to defy the arid conditions and share their spoils.

For it has always been about knowing where the water is: and it's no less so today.

On the southern rim of the Basin you'll find the Marree Yacht Club, a surprising find, given the reputation the Lake has of filling up so infrequently. Yet this is no tourist gimmick set up with an eye to the tourist market, but a serious affair started by a couple of salties from Melbourne who just wanted to get reliable information about the Lake.

"We get a sail somewhere on the Lake about every two or three years," one of the founders tells me. "There's always water somewhere in the Basin. This year I was able to do a river sail, and I went down the Warburton for the third time. And the Kallakoopah was flowing for the first time since 2000 so I was able to do a loop."

We're talking at the Yacht Club as he shows me the photographic display of the Lake in water. There are pictures dating back several decades of yachties sailing on the Lake, and he tells me there is first-hand evidence of the Lake being sailed from the nineteen-fifties, with claims going back even further. But the hapless explorer Sturt must qualify as the first Lake Eyre "Gunna", with his 1840s effort to lug a whaleboat in to sail the "inland sea", only to abandon it when he failed to find the water.

But many of the more impressive pictures of the Lake are without water, the stark and eerie landscape catching the light like no other place I've seen, even showing the salty surface to be a rich pink at times.

"That's caused by the beta-Carotene pigment in the salt*," the co-founder explains. "It also produces glycerine that makes the water very oily, so it's like you're sailing on a sea of pink oil.

"And at times the evaporation is so strong it causes an updraft that actually deflects the prevailing wind up, so you can get becalmed in the middle of the Lake.

"It's really not like sailing anywhere else in the world."

This claim is supported by the many sailors who come from all corners of the globe for the chance to experience these phenomena. But there are cautions for the inexperienced. Even when there is sailable water in the Lake, reaching it may involve a long drive across an unreliable salt crust that can give way at any time. And bogged in the black ooze beneath the crust would be no dignified place for a sailor to be.

"Most people don't realize just how big the Lake is," the co-founder continues. "Even a minor flooding can produce more sailable water than Port Phillip Bay has. In all the time I've been

* Produced by the algae *Dunaliella salina*. For example see photo, colour section one, page 1, top.

sailing on the Lake I've never seen another boat. Which tends to make you pretty spoilt."

"It's just so peaceful as it is, so beautiful; I wouldn't like to think what I'd do if I ever saw jet skis on the Lake."

I ask him if he gets many disappointed tourists towing their boats all the way from their homes on the coast, only to find there's not enough water in the Lake to sail.

"We get some, but they're usually philosophical about it. This year we even bought a couple of boats off them. We get 'em pretty cheap when they're in the middle of the desert," he laughs.

So be warned.

A LONG WAY TO THE TOP

One of the more enduring debates in this country has been whether or not we should climb Uluru. Some believe we should leave it to the traditional owners (the Anangu people) who've been quoted for some time as saying they'd rather we didn't climb. Others feel just as strongly that Ayres Rock is for everyone to enjoy and the blackfellas don't have a mortgage on spiritual ties with the land. Another camp perhaps wonders if they're careful to always call it Uluru and buy a souvenir from the shop would it be okay if they sneaked up in their socks, just this once with the kids before it does get closed?

Fact is it's our most contentious icon and it probably doesn't do us any harm to reconsider our relationship with it every so often. I'd even go so far as to say it's something of a litmus test for our dealings with our indigenous community.

It's currently under the joint control of Uluru-Kata Tjuta Board of Management made up of both Anangu and non-Anangu representatives, and National Parks Australia. (Although it would be naïve to imagine bodies such as the Central Land Council and even non-related Federal Government departments wouldn't occasionally stick their noses in.)

When the Director of National Parks recently released the Draft Management Plan for 2009-19 it ignited a furor over the possibility "the walk" would no longer be allowed, and called for public comment.

Naturally the media pounced on the story – television networks had very important journalists climbing all over it, radio jocks nationwide had an original talkback topic for a whole week and newspapers ran the story nationwide – yet I read (most of) the document in question and found little serious indication there was to be any change to the *status quo*.

The section of the document that sparked the furor was hardly inflammatory. It defined the spiritual significance of "the climb" to the traditional owners as one that should only be undertaken by a wallaby (few who've done it would argue), and addressed the duty of care concerns the original custodians have regarding the health and safety risks. Thirty-odd people have died climbing The

Rock since the practice began (in significant numbers probably not till the nineteen-seventies), and the document hinted without actually saying as much that the overweight and unfit would soon be actively discouraged from taking the climb (might I suggest a doughnut stand at the base?). And by way of a definitive conclusion it proposed that steps might probably be taken in the not too distant future to maybe one day close the climb altogether. Possibly.

Of course I'm being flippant (not to mention politically incorrect at every turn), and I've no doubt Mala the ancestral Hare-wallaby is an important part of the aboriginal story for some, just as I accept many Anangu people genuinely fear for our safety. But let's not get blinded by our desire to see.

In my experience with our Aborigines they are about as welcoming as any group of human beings in the world, and providing you respect their (relatively few) wishes regarding their sacred sites and rituals they will extend levels of generosity rarely seen in white society. They don't embrace the same concept of ownership that we do, and the very notion of them calling the shots regarding "the climb" is anathema to their thinking. The prevailing attitude I've struck seems to be "okay, go ahead if you need to; who am I to stop you?" Indeed many I've spoken to aren't precious about the issue at all; they *do* think we're mad for climbing, but only because "there's nothing up there", not because it offends their spiritual sensibilities.

There is a perception in "enlightened" urban Australia that rural Australians are rednecks who don't understand the aboriginal condition, which, of course, is sophist nonsense. Indeed when the latest government initiative collapses in a shamble of wasted funds and jobs for the boys, when the health system fails to reach those in dire need, or perhaps most tragically when even the organizations run *by* Aborigines *for* Aborigines succumb to the same fat cat ideology as any other public service department, it is often the local communities that deal with the fallout, and feed and medicate the black kids living on their properties and take up their cause with the holders of the purse.

Similarly there is a tendency for urban Australia to clamour for justice when it comes to Aboriginal issues, to see only the "give it back" argument and reject all others as racist, yet how many would be so benevolent if the land claim included their own property in the suburbs? And let's face it; if we are to adopt the argument that Uluru be returned to its traditional owners on the grounds that *they were there first,* then logic demands we also accept that argument for all of Australia. But we all know the red centre of the country is a long way from the warm glow of the suburbs.

(By the way, I'm not saying there is no racism in the bush – it's no less prevalent than it is in the cities and a damn sight more obvious – but it's country people who live at the coalface of this issue and usually know a thing or two about what's happening out there. Consequently their opinions aren't as academic as those of the enlightened southerner: they're more organic, and as real as the sight of hungry black kids sitting beside their mothers in the street waiting for them to sleep it off.)

Meanwhile the debate gets re-ignited every time a new Management Plan hits the table or an old ideology finds fresh voice in a new vocal minority, and with each round it seems the hope of a harmonious outcome ebbs a little further away and we move a little closer to a segregated Australia where black and white don't share or, ultimately, perhaps inevitably, even mix.

There are no easy solutions to the Aboriginal problems in this country and anyone who thinks otherwise isn't thinking. But to my mind there are better ways to spend our energies than to argue about climbing a rock in the middle of the country. After all, how can it possibly matter in the real scheme of things, or perhaps better *the scheme of real things*, whether or not we continue an activity that causes no serious harm to anyone but ourselves?

So if it pleases you get out there and climb the bloody thing, I say. The moral high horse doesn't carry much weight over the long haul. If, on the other hand, you choose to heed the wishes of the Anangu and not climb, then good for you. But either way you go, get involved, know what you're doing and why you're doing it. As I see it there is no absolute right or wrong here, only a long way to go before we can hope to start sharing this country as equals.

CAMELS, PROMOMAN AND THE YEPERENYE

The first camel to arrive in Australia came from Tenerife in 1840 and was called Harry. He was a spirited rogue and way too fond of biting for his own good, but it wasn't till he killed his handler – by bumping him while he was loading his muscat, causing the gun to discharge in his face and subsequent death by gangrene –

that it was decided Harry had to go. Before he died his handler ordered Harry be put down, not out of revenge, he insisted, but because he was not a good specimen to breed from.

Undeterred by Harry's example, Australia continued to import camels for use, especially, in the exploration and development of the central desert regions. When the motor vehicle was introduced in the 1920s there were 20,000 in the country, most of which were set free to fend for themselves. And fend they did in no shy way and today it's estimated there is roughly a million feral camels roaming the interior of Australia, a number expected to double within the decade. Not only does this pose a problem for pastoralists trying to raise cattle on marginal land, but it's also a serious environmental threat.

It's appropriate that I'm looking at the camel story while I'm stuck in Alice Springs, which owes a great debt to the 'Afghan' led camel trains that opened up the north-south link between Darwin and Adelaide. (In reality most of the cameleers weren't really Afghans at all but, Pakistanis from the *then* British India). But to be honest if I had the choice of where to be broken down awaiting parts in the Northern Territory I'd choose Darwin every time, not least because air freight for the parts I'm waiting on from the east comes via Darwin anyway.

However I have an ebullient mate living in Alice Springs who won't hear of it. He's something of an unofficial promotional machine for the place. Mention you'll get something fixed in Darwin and he'll railroad you to an Alice supplier before you've finished the sentence. Casually refer to the place as "the middle of nowhere" and he'll pounce on you every time.

"It's the middle of Australia," he'll correct. "Closest town to every beach in the country. Great climate. Fantastic people. Why would anyone live anywhere else?"

He's not being arrogant. Just can't help himself. He's a true believer, loves the place. And drives me nuts in the process.

Don't get me wrong. I don't mind The Alice, for her friendly people and dry river charm, or the Red Centre for its space and vibrant colours. I just prefer not to have to endure a sermon every time I visit. But now I was trapped for two weeks or more and Promoman set to work.

"The *yeperenye's* got you," he informed me early on.

"What's that?'

"The local dreaming, mate. Caterpillar dreaming. Those of us lucky enough to call Alice Springs home *belongem yeperenye.*"

"What sort of caterpillar?"

"*Yeperenye* caterpillar. And once he gets in you can never leave."

"No chance, Promoman. Soon as these parts arrive I'm gone."

But that didn't deter him one iota. He arranged drinks with some locals, including a couple of friendly women. "See that?" he said quietly at one point, indicating the women. "That's the *yeperenye* at work."

He's a clown, is Promoman. But I was getting the idea.

In essence *yeperenye* is one of three caterpillars regarded as important totems for the *Arrente* people of Alice Springs. To paraphrase the story as I understand it the *yeperenye* emerged from the ground at Emily Gap into the waiting claws of the stink beetle, which set about nipping off the caterpillars' heads and spreading their guts all over the ground. Somehow a few *yeperenye* managed to survive the massacre, and subsequent encounters with its other enemy the wild dog, and crawl away to form the Macdonnell Ranges that surround the town – a mighty effort for the decapitated larvae of the humble hawk moth. But serious students of Aboriginal culture would be well advised to do their own research on this, and the many other wonderful stories from the region.

Most of my research was being directed towards Claude. The brake problem had escalated into a major issue with the disc rotors, the auto-electrics were in disarray, and disappointingly my supplier* was doing a Houdini and refusing to take any responsibility. From that point our relationship soured and I was flying solo in a fully imported hybrid 4x4 that nobody had ever heard of.

"*Yeperenye*," said Promoman, when I informed him of yet another delay. "Let me introduce you to my real estate agent."

And so it was in the middle of this enforced stay in The Alice I decided to do a hot lap of the Red Centre, with Promoman for company. I wanted to follow the camel story and shoot some vision for Tourism Australia, and Promoman wanted to drink beer with anyone he could find *en route*. I left a day early to pick up Chambers Pillar and Rainbow Valley on the way; Promoman was to meet me at The Rock.

But there are a lot of rocks in the NT and most of them aren't tourist attractions. A goodly number you'll find on the way out to

* Only common decency prevents me naming this company.

Chambers Pillar, for instance, in the middle of the road. In fact sometimes that's the only way you can tell the difference, they're so big. That, and the fact there aren't doe-eyed tourists camped at their base.

I'm afraid something terrible happens to people with too much time and too little to see: they become rock-worshippers. And once they set up camp and plonk their bums in foldaway chairs, favourite tipple in hand, their eyes glaze over like born-agains and the world becomes a beautiful big thing. They've probably spent their entire working lives chasing deadlines and now they scorn anyone – like me, for instance – who rushes in and out without stopping for at least one sunset to fully appreciate the majesty of the rock/pillar/falls/escarpment in focus. And they're probably justified in their thinking, but I think rock formations in Central Australia are a bit like castles in Europe: after the first two I'd rather be drinking something unpronounceable in the local tavern.

At Rainbow Valley – yet another rock feature with a torturous access road – I catch up with a cameleer I'd met in The Alice. He operates a camel ride business, one of tourism's growth industries over the past ten years, and looks like Tom Petty without his Heartbreakers.

He tells me all the camels in Australia today are descendents of the original stocks from the post-Harry period, and they're considered the world's healthiest population of dromedary camels (one humped; the bactrian has two).

"It's an ideal environment for them here. Australia's got the most vegetated deserts in the world, and camels keep moving and graze on a wide variety of feed, so they don't tend to threaten individual plant species.

"In addition they've got soft feet like our native animals, so they cause far less damage to the topsoil than cattle and horses and the like."

Which makes them sound like an ideal feral resource to harvest to me, and a former National Parks ranger I meet later on agrees, though he's less convinced about their footprint on the environment.

"That's the impact of camel grazing you can see there," he says, pointing out some scrub where the vegetation has been stripped bare below about camel-height. "So it's not hard to imagine what they'll do if their numbers keep rising. And they're difficult to contain because they'll walk straight through stock fences."

But he doesn't agree with injudicious culling.

"A fully-grown adult camel weighs in at around 600kgs, and the carcass dresses down to about half that weight. So that's a lot of protein to be dropping in the desert and leaving to rot.

"They're a tricky animal to muster because they're so mobile and you can clean out an area one day and come back the next to find more camels have drifted in. But if we gave them a dollar value we might see co-operation between stations and get something done."

"Are they harder to muster in the winter when they need less water?"

"No. The main problem with wintertime is it's the middle of the breeding cycle and the bulls stink. They stand with their legs apart and urinate backwards onto their tail, then flick it all over their back. It's quite a pungent smell. We call it Camel No. 5."

Meanwhile I'd collected Promoman at The Rock and stopped for a beer with every human being over the age of eighteen between there and Kings Canyon. At some point we decided to take the Mereenie Loop back to The Alice, an idea that proved less than sound. I know it's perilous to comment on road conditions in this country since they can change as quickly as the road is graded, but at the time of travel this one was simply murderous. Claude barely made it back at all, never mind in one piece (one of his Mickey Mouse ears flapped right off, among other things).

But driving through Albert Namitjira* country made it *almost* worth the carnage, at times feeling like we were *in* one of his landscape paintings the terrain was so true to his brush. Promoman was in raptures, and with every change of vista he'd come out with something like, "Fantastic country. Why would you live anywhere else?"

He was giving me the shits so I changed the subject. Promoman owns a restaurant that serves camel and I asked him how it went down with the punters.

"It's bloody beautiful, mate, leanest meat in the world. The steak cuts taste just like beef, and the butt has all the flavours of a roast lamb, so we call it Jurassic Lamb Shank on the menu. It serves a hundred and the tourists love it."

* Australian Aboriginal artist who excelled in landscapes, particularly of the West MacDonnell ranges, who is credited with being the first aboriginal artist to paint in a western style. This point of reference aside, his work was exceptional in its own right, capturing the light and colours of the region as few have done before or since.

"Do you eat it?"

"Of course! That's why I'm in such good physical condition, mate." Promoman's built like Homer Simpson only marginally less athletic. He may drive me nuts but I still find him amusing.

Back at The Alice my parts had arrived and I was soon ready to push on. I touched base with Tourism Australia and told them I had enough vision to cut a good little segment on the Red Centre. That's when I learned I wouldn't be able to use the footage because they didn't issue filming permits post-production. I'd have to return at a later stage to do it all again.

"No worries, mate. That's just the *yeperenye*."

ALIEN VISITATIONS

"You feel very uneasy when you get the close encounters," he tells me, opening up another image on his computer screen, "because you know they're not of this world."

"Do you ever get scared?"

"Shit, yeah," he says with some force. "I was sitting out under the verandah one night when a shadow fell on the yard, and I was too frightened to even look up. There was something just above the tree line, but I couldn't bring myself to look. The dog saw it, looked right at it, then back at me. But I couldn't move. I was terrified!"

The look on his face is as real as if he'd just seen it again over my shoulder.

I had this exchange with a keen UFO hunter I met just south of Darwin, who'd recently been the focus of a media-frenzy when one of his photographs made front page of the local newspaper. The NT News is notorious for publishing outlandish stories. Anything crocodile-related will usually get a run, a talking cat is excellent grist, headlines like "Authorities Plead – Stop Having Sex in Public" are not uncommon and alien stories are par for the course. Often the quirk-hungry southern media will pick them and give them a run, and this ufologist – *their* term, by the way, not mine – was hot property for a week or two on the strength of his exposure.

So much so, that between contacting him and the agreed interview time he lost his enthusiasm for doing the story and tried to renege. I asked him if he'd been treated well by the media so far.

"Yeah, most of them have been okay. One guy from Melbourne started the interview by saying 'only farmers and rednecks see UFOs; which one was I?' but overall they've been good. I just don't want to give too much away. I want to save some for my book."

In the end we agreed he could pull his punches wherever he pleased and I'd be happy to work with whatever crumbs he threw me. And when it came down to it he was more than generous, anyway.

I met him at his local pub, but he decided to take me to his home to give me the full picture. Most of the story was supported by images on his computer and without seeing the evidence he didn't think I'd get the full impact of what he was doing. He was right. Sitting beside him at the computer screen it was hard not to be infected by his enthusiasm and start believing in a world of spaceships and aliens.

"How it all started was when I was taking shots of the clouds, skyscapes you know, because the colours in the clouds turn me on. And when I zoomed them up on the screen I'd sometimes see spots in the background, different shapes and sizes.

"So the early shots were all flukes. But then I started seeing them with my own eyes, silver flashes and dots in the sky, and I started concentrating on busting the aliens."

He laughs when he says this, aware of how ludicrous it might sound to a newbie like me. In fact he laughs at himself a lot, which makes it easier to enjoy his story whether you believe him or not. And the shots he brings up on screen certainly add credibility. The UFOs are rarely centre frame, as if captured by happenstance rather than design, and they do indeed come in all shapes and sizes.

Some take on the classical flying saucer shape – a disc with a bulbous centre – others look more like a cigar with one shiny end reflecting the sunlight, and at least one looks more like a flying saucepan than a flying saucer and I wonder if I'm not experiencing visual dyslexia.

"Most of them look like they're about twenty metres across, but this one was much bigger," he says, zooming into a triangular-shaped black spot on the luminous edge of a backlit storm cloud. "I think it might be a mother ship."

"And *what* is *that*?" I ask him about one shaped like a cat's eye burr, the kind you'd get stuck in your bare feet in the summer.

"I don't know. I really don't know. Some people think it looks like a helicopter, but it doesn't look like any helicopter I've ever seen. Have you ever seen one like that?"

I shake my head. The cat's eye image is very clear, with three prongs extending from a triangular body: two at the front, one longer one at the tail. For want of a better description it looks like a space ship designed for a stick figure sci-fi.

Another one is shaped more like a teardrop with a white head and on its flank he points out a shaded area he thinks could be a bank of windows. There's not enough detail for me to make a conclusion one way or another but there's definitely something odd about the external texture. And it's clearly not a speck of dust on the lens. Like most of his images there's no doubt it has three dimensions, and it seems to have been caught, as he puts it, "doing whatever it is they do". There's no question it's a UFO, regardless of whatever else it may or may not be.

"And the thing about all these UFOs is they don't make a sound, not one sound.

"And they're only ever in shot for one frame. If it's a bird or a plane they'll be in shot for a couple of frames before and after, but not these.

"One of the interviewers asked me why the air force doesn't just shoot them out of the sky, but they wouldn't have a hope. They're too fast, and they zip about the place like nothing we can match. There's just no comparison."

"Is there a time when they're more active?"

"Yeah, during military exercises and during the wet season buildup. And they seem to hang around power stations as well. Water, power and the military."

He's a likable bloke in his forties who you wouldn't think to question on any other topic. Even when he does skate well out on the thin ice I don't feel the need to stamp my feet: he's too good-natured. At one stage he tells me he believes "they know he knows" and I suggest he might be the chosen one, that they're coming to get him. He just laughs and says he hopes I'm wrong.

But fear of abduction never stopped a good ufologist. When he feels the time is right he goes out to one of his preferred spots and watches, sometimes for hours, and when the flashes start he starts shooting. He operates a simple Canon Proshot 8 megapixel stills camera for most of his work, either hand-held or off a tripod. He also has some video footage of "his boys", but the best examples I saw were still shots.

"I spend hours scanning and erasing shots. I've deleted thousands and thousands, literally.

"That's what's made the difference: digital photography, and the computer. The UFOs have probably always been there, but before digital it was almost impossible to catch them the way I do. But now you can go out and take a few hundred shots and delete all but the ones you want, then blow them up on the screen to see what you've got."

And what he's got is a fairly compelling body of evidence, although he knows most people will remain skeptical unless they see one with their own eyes.

"I was a bit that way myself," he admits. "I used to drive past Wycliffe Well* there and think he must be crackers. Especially since he's got the most varieties of beer in the Territory. But he's seen them. And now I've seen them for myself I'm convinced.

"You get sucked in. Once you bust a few aliens you want to bust more. It's a different kind of photography. Way out there, you know?

"I'm just like you," he tells me. "I started out taking pictures of clouds and now I've lost the plot and I'm chasing aliens. You started out doing the weather now you've lost the plot and you're travelling around the country. So it's all got something to do with the weather, hasn't it?"

* A roadhouse located 130kms south of Tennant Creek in the Northern Territory, self-named the UFO capital of Australia because of the regular sightings claimed by the owner. For more information on aliens in the NT go to www.ufoterritory.com.au

THE MUSTER

It was all too early. I never quite woke up. The Boss was feeling fragile. The night before had taken its toll, but there was a muster on and it would have been churlish of me to decline the offer.

There are four choppers on the muster and flying to the job the radio chat keeps us amused. One pilot claims to be afraid of heights and it's hard to know how much of that absurdity is real and how much is for the jest. Another has just returned from a few days leave in Darwin and the boys rib him about his strike rate with the girls. Below us the land rushes past at a hundred miles an hour in reds and greens and browns, over plains and ups and downs.

In spite of the radio contact we have trouble re-grouping once we reach the job site: a small helicopter is not an easy thing to spot in the vastness, either against the sky or the land, and one of the pilots is way off course. Indeed it all looks the same to me – the trees, the ridges, even the river courses – and I'm rarely the first to spot another chopper. After about half an hour the wayward pilot is guided back to the fold and the muster begins.

To the untrained eye it looks like random flying across featureless terrain, but slowly it comes together, gradually the detail emerges.

The radio chat is constant and offers a clearer picture than my eyes can deliver. As one pilot said to me later, "We see with our ears."

"Where are you now, Scotty?" The Boss says over the radio.

"Working that country to the west of the junction there," comes the reply. "Got a few bulls coming out of the timber. Fat, they are, too."

The Boss seems satisfied with his answer though I've got no idea where the junction is – in fact I'm having trouble enough keeping track of the compass points – but I can see the bulls in my mind's eye, imagine them running from the noise of the chopper, rolling haunches glistening in the morning sun.

We flush out a few bulls of our own: a motley Brahman-cross

and a red bull with a gammy back leg. They run together like best mates and look like they've been through the drill before. We bank and pivot around a tree and they lope from underneath it but only as far as the next stand of trees. They look up at us waiting for our next move. The Boss leaves them, for now.

A mob of six or eight cows and calves scatter along a sandy creek bank and we wheel them around and through its dry bed. They come out the other side and head across the flat in the right direction, dust kicking up from their heels. The Boss peels away.

A lone bull wants to have a go and stands defiant, snorting and tossing his horns, but the din of the chopper bearing down proves all too much and he turns and gallops across the flat towards the mob. Again The Boss breaks away, eyes scanning the land ahead looking for movement where it shouldn't be, colour where it doesn't belong.

"Got anything down your way, Steven?"

"Yeah, got a little mob travelin' now, maybe forty or so,' comes the deep-voiced reply. "Just headin' back to refuel."

"Don't suppose you brought any coffee?"

"I'll leave it at the drop."

"That's the one," says The Boss, and his demeanor visibly lifts as we change direction towards the fuel dump.

And as the morning wears a pattern emerges. The cattle are finessed from the timber in ones and twos and small mobs and pushed towards the river. Small mobs join others and form numbers "travelling". Sometimes donkeys or camels get caught in the mix but they rarely stick. Horses run like the wind but never look like joining the herd. Bustards labour in flight below, trying to escape the noise. And the choppers whirr and buzz overhead, working the flanks of a map that exists only in the pilot's mind. It's a wild and tenuous interfacing.

The Boss lands on a ridge and points out over the plain to the dust coming off the herd several kilometres distant. It seems like some kind of minor miracle to me that what we've been doing in the choppers has caused this effect. A mob of about eighty or a hundred cattle is running towards the yard they've set up along the river.

"They're travellin' good now. We'll leave them be. Want more coffee?"

We drink and enjoy standing on firm ground for a moment, grateful for the absence of movement if not a full coffee-lead recovery, before we're in the air again. An hour or two of looking into the camera's viewfinder hasn't improved my disposition, and The Boss looks like eating a green apple would finish him off for good.

The separate mobs are reaching the river now and the choppers are pushing them along its banks. It's more exacting flying than out on the plains, with the pilots often working together in-between the trees. The communication on the radio becomes more serious.

"Right on your tail, Scotty. Don't come back."

"Rightooooooo. Where are you Mick?"

"Just above you to the west. Got a few cattle along that little feeder creek there. Hold up and I'll run 'em in to you."

“Rightooooooo. Swinging left now Steve.”

“I see you.”

And the choppers dip and weave through the timber, sometimes even dropping out of sight below the treetops, working so close at times it looks impossible they can avoid touching. It’s like watching some crazy aerial ballet choreographed by a thrill seeker with an eye for detail.

And the mob keeps “travellin’ good.”

From the air the trap is obvious. The portable yards are set up on a narrow flat between the ranges and the river. Funneling the cattle into the yards are two fenced “wings” angled inwards to the opening. The fences are draped in hessian to stop the stock galloping right through, and one runs from the yards to the slopes while the other crosses the dry riverbed and fans out over the lightly timbered scrub on the other side. There is always stock left behind in a muster – rogue bulls that know the ropes, cleanskins caught in pockets of thick scrub, our gammy bull and his mate – but few get missed within sight of the yards.

By the time the mob hits the trap the dust is thick and the choppers are four deep in the sky. A small mob breaks to the wing and a chopper peels away and drives them back through the sandy riverbed and up the other side. He pirouettes in their wake and scoops the chopper up and over the trees at the last second as another chopper slips in behind him to keep the stragglers moving. The radio is in constant use now and you can hear the tension in their exchanges, the excitement in their voices. Too much pressure in the wrong direction at this point could scatter the mob and add an hour or two to the job. On the ground the farmers are driving their utes slowly down the other wing, making sure the cattle don't overrun the opening and head up the slope. You can sense the end.

Then the lead cattle start trampling into the yard and it is all but over. Providing the musterers keep their distance the rest of the mob will follow. The Boss climbs high over the scene to do a rough count.

"A couple of hundred head, there. Maybe three. Would've thought we'd get more." Then he changes course. "You sort that out on the ground, Steven?"

"Will do. You not going down?"

"Gotta get back. Things to do."

The Boss throws me a knowing look as we make a beeline for the refueling dump. I've felt queasier in my time, but I really don't remember when.

FLYING LIZARDS

"I lose about fifty head of cattle a year to the big crocs," The Boss tells me. "But he'll only eat the nose and maybe a hoof or two. Then he'll sit on the rest of the carcass and pick off the turtles and catfish and kites that come to feed off it. He likes fresh meat."

I had no idea they were so smart and say as much.

"They're smart all right. To give you an example that bullock carcass I showed you in the water today was killed by a croc about sixteen foot long, and last time I flew over he was lying up next to it. So I put the chopper down to get a better look at him but by the time I'd walked back he'd moved off it a bit and he ambushed me on the way. Exploded out of the water and lunged at me. Just about had me, too. Only thing that saved me was the bank being about a metre high there in that spot.

"He was fishing, using that beast as his bait, waiting for a pig or a dingo or me to come along. I've got goose bumps just thinkin' about it."

This is not a man prone to histrionics or exaggeration and the more I listen to him the more I'm inclined to believe him. Crocs have a reputation for lardering their food, but I always thought it was to allow a kill to rot so it could be more readily broken up. But it doesn't stand to reason an animal at the top of the food chain would eat rotten meat unless it had no choice. And it's no quantum leap to believe they're smart enough to use a dead beast as a trap for fresh game.

The man I'm talking to owns a cattle station in the western Top End, where they seem to use choppers for everything. They use them for contract mustering to flush out the cattle in country the motorbikes and horses can't handle. They use them for collecting crocodile eggs from the floodplains in the wet season. They use them to spot fire the National Parks as part of their fire management plan. And I've no doubt they even get used for shopping trips to Darwin, on occasion.

Not everybody uses the choppers, of course. There are plenty of cowboys around using cars and quad bikes and even horses, for heaven's sake how very quaint. But since I'm a guest of The Boss and he's a chopper guy, I'm a chopper guy, too.

I have an old friend (both meanings) from Darwin accompanying me on this leg and he's now a confirmed chopper guy as well, after taking his maiden flight here. We flew down the Victoria River to set a few crocodile traps and he was instantly converted. Admittedly it's a beautiful river and there's no better way to see the country than from a chopper. My mate got so excited that last night he drank to excess and thanked our hosts many times in 'Swahili'. I've taken to calling him Wamboobi, after a Kenyan I once knew who almost got me killed by a Somalian princess … but that's another story: this one's about helicopters and crocodiles, choppers and lizards.

The Boss here has evolved croc trapping to an art form. He uses similar traps to the standard floating affairs you see all over Darwin Harbour, only his are lighter and more portable and he doesn't have to get out of his chopper to set them. He flies the baited trap to the desired location with a grappling hook on a chain beneath the chopper, then sets it down at the edge of the water and releases it.

Then when he catches a croc he picks the whole package up with the grappling hook and carries it to a place more suitable for getting angry crocodiles from traps than the water's edge – the last place you want to be concentrating on a trapped man-eater is in the vicinity of liberated man-eaters.

After we set the traps we do a short reccy to look for the big croc, but see only smaller crocs including a couple of three metre specimens with peculiar white heads, just downstream from the bullock carcass.

"That's bullock fat," The Boss explains. "They've had their heads up the arse of that beast.

"But they'll only feed off it during the daytime. The big fella'll kill them if they try it on at night."

To illustrate his point there's small crocodile carcass floating upside down not far from the dead bullock, almost certainly killed by the big croc.

The two white-headed crocs look likely candidates for the traps and we decide to wait an hour or two so we can check the traps just before dark. To pass the time we go barra fishing.

Barra fishing chopper-style involves flying over a hole in the river and spotting how many big fish are in it, then landing and catching them. Simple as that. We fly over one with three big fish and land and catch exactly that: three big fish. I think our combined casts total ten in about as many minutes. I can't in all honesty say it was the most satisfying fishing I've ever done but it was certainly effective. And they tasted just as good as fish I've worked hard for.

But the white-headed crocs prove cagier than we thought and the traps are empty when we check them on the run home, though we're confident we'll have at least one by the next morning.

We're wrong. The next day not only are the traps still empty, but the bullock carcass is gone as well.

"The big croc probably moved it somewhere else last night," is The Boss's take, "because we were buggering about setting traps here, too much activity."

We do a run downstream to see if we can spot where he's taken it. Flying at a hundred feet the river comes to life in rushes. Startled cormorants stay with us for frantic bursts before crashing into the water at speed like front row forwards hitting the line. Jabirus rise from the shallows trailing their long legs as they peel away, smooth as flowing cream. A flock of corellas crosses the river and for a moment the clear green water is pockmarked white with their reflections. Wily crocodiles floating midstream, heads above the surface and bodies dangling below at the laziest of angles, sink without trace before we reach them, while others basking in the shallows bolt to the deeper water in powerful bursts. But there's no sign of the big croc or his "trap". The Boss looks thoughtful as we leave the river.

Wamboobi and I are thoughtful, too, after seeing a number of sizeable crocs scramble through the shallow water. The night before we'd camped at the old river crossing and assumed because there was no deep water in the vicinity we were beyond the reach of crocodiles. So we'd bathed in the calf-deep rapids and collected water for the billy several times through the night without concern; from what we'd saw from the chopper it was unlikely we'd be so cavalier again.*

Meanwhile, back at the station, the next morning we get a result. We don't catch the sixteen-footer but one of the white-headed crocs is waiting in the trap when we arrive. It's the female of the

* Wamboobi and I camped at the same location on return from the Kimberleys, though this time we treated the water with more respect. It was a great setting (see photo, colour section two, page 1, bottom) and since it was our last night on the road together we set up camp early and drank to the success of the trip as we watched the setting sun paint the escarpment red. It was a grand party for two, and although we saw no crocs, towards dusk we did see more light aircraft flying in from the north than had any right doing. Later we were told by someone who should know, that the Victoria River is often used as a landmark for aircraft entering the country illegally, though Wamboobi wasn't entirely convinced they weren't aliens coming to collect him.

pair, and she'll be sold to a croc farm in Darwin as a breeder. There's good money in eggs to supply the skin and meat trade and she'll lay about forty eggs a year for the next thirty years, earning her keep many times over.

While the fly-in-and-drop method is an efficient way to catch crocs, at some stage the reptile still has to be manhandled out of the trap, and as you can probably imagine they're not happy about it. The first stage involves slipping a wire noose over the animal's snout and dragging it from the trap, and appears to require equal parts luck, finesse and bravado. Then once the croc is removed it's wrapped in heavy rope netting and flown beneath the chopper to a holding pen at the homestead. For me the two highlights of the procedure were: firstly, when Wamboobi threw his aging frame on the animal's back, grey pigtail flying behind him like a contrail from a jet and looking for all the world like a stuntman from Dad's Army; and secondly, seeing the white underbelly of the animal silhouetted* against a vivid blue sky as it was being choppered back to the homestead. Nice moments.

That night over a few beers the culling issue comes up. Since hunting was outlawed back in the seventies Territory crocodile number have risen from about five thousand to an estimated seventy-five thousand, and a number of recent fatal attacks had evoked the usual hue and cry.

"Yeah, trapping's the way to go," The Boss reckons. "With trophy hunting you never really know whether you've got the animal or not, but this way you see the animal, you set the trap, you catch him. Just like the barramundi." I remind him the sixteen-footer's still out there but he doesn't thank me for it.

*See photo, colour section two, page 4, top.

"We better get a couple more beers, eh?" is how he responds instead.

KILLING WAMBOOBI

Wamboobi introduces himself to the other guests as my artistic director, a role he embellishes as the night stakes its claim. He has at least one couple convinced he plays the fiddle and does an Irish jig at the start of my segments. They are impressed, if a little bemused. I overhear another woman asking him if he's ever worked with Nicole Kidman. He is modest in assent. There's no doubting he's in excellent form, but water always finds its own level.

We are at Faraway Bay, an up-market bush camp on the north Kimberley coast. Our hosts are a congenial couple who've seen it all before: the holiday desperados stuffing themselves with as much escape as they can harness, the raconteurs and charmers taking advantage of a captive audience, the drunks enraptured by the open bar. I'm only mildly concerned about the damage my old friend could wreak.

Earlier that day we visited an aboriginal art site to see the Bradshaw paintings*, rock art so old even the aboriginals didn't recognize it.

*See photo, colour section two, page 3, top.

"They don't know the stories behind this art," our guide tells us. "So there's no oral tradition.

Indeed up until about twenty years ago many indigenous people still rejected it as "rubbish painting" and the work of the birds, thought the red was bloodstains from their beaks. Yet others insist the bird is an integral part of the story and have therefore embraced the style, and would argue they always did. And there is further debate over whether Bradshaw art is Gwion Gwion art, or the latter merely a copy of the former.

What isn't in doubt in my mind is it's different to any Australian rock art I've seen before, more sophisticated, with finer brushwork and often greatly stylized form; I saw one abstracted female figure with a metre-long body and pencil-thin arms, with huge hands extending well beyond her feet. I've seen European masters' work in a similar vein.

But it's the decorations that truly set them apart.

"See the arm bands and bangles on her wrists, and braids and tassles in her hair," our guide points out, referring to a well-preserved and very elegantly drawn figure. "That's classic Bradshaw."

Joseph Bradshaw was a pastoralist who came to the Kimberley to run cattle, only to find the country too rocky for that purpose. Instead he occupied himself documenting the rock art and talking to the aboriginal people about its origins. It was he who first recorded their reactions and it's not hard to see why they dismissed the art as they did.

"Notice the ornamentation hanging off her skirt? Sometimes it looks like they've got animals in their headdresses. More African than Australian Aborigine."

I can tell Wamboobi approves of this idea by the haughty look he's wearing. He still deludes himself that his British heritage gives him proprietorial rights in the old colonies, Africa included, and he probably imagines he had something to do with it.

He was fond of saying, "When we gave you Australia two hundred years ago it was a magnificent country; now look what you've done with it." But a man in our group who speaks in a monotonous drone through the side of his mouth suggests we look north for inspiration, with a nod to the Papua New Guinean habit of carrying their pets in their hair.

"The paintings are upwards of about twelve thousand years old," our guide continues, "some say as old as fifty thousand. They don't really know because the pigment has penetrated the sandstone and can't be carbon dated."

Wamboobi changes tack.

"These paintings were quite clearly done by the aliens," he says with a wave to the heavens. "My people."

It's unlikely the gathered throng has a clue what he's talking about but they laugh anyway and the droning stops. And the art does have an otherworldly feel about it and surely questions conventional wisdom about who our original inhabitants were. I make a vow to use the term 'previous custodians' rather than 'original custodians' in future, since it's clear to me there were others came before.

The droner has something to say on the matter of art preservation but we can't hear what it is.

"That man sounds like a didgeridoo," Wamboobi observes.

Back in camp that night the Bradshaws are discussed again,

though mainly by The Human Didgeridoo as he's now commonly known. But Wamboobi has moved on to more challenging projects. He's discovered a sizeable cherubin in the fish tank and fancies it as *hors d'oeuvre*. Fortunately dinner is served before he can work out how to catch the thing.

Including staff there's about twenty of us dining and it's a pleasantly cordial affair. Wamboobi has found himself a Mauritian drinking partner, which should keep him from goading the Human Didgeridoo all night and might even save the cherubin. Once I finish my meal I leave him to it and hope for the best. He returns to our cabin late and proclaims the night was such a great success it will go down in the "anuses of history", then promptly falls asleep.

The next morning I learn he was found in the garden with his arms around the Human Didgeridoo, "helping each other home," he assures me. But since nothing seems amiss at breakfast I don't ask for details and he doesn't volunteer them. Sometimes it's better that way.

Our outing for the day is to King George Gorge, a spectacular waterway carved into the sandstone by millions of years of wet season rains thundering over the escarpment. According to our host the falls featured in the movie Australia, though the water had to be added during post-production since they filmed it in the dry season.

That night is much like the previous one, only when Wamboobi staggers in he wants to talk literature. On my recommendation he has read The Road by Cormac McCarthy – a bleak and beautiful work by a master at the height of his powers, which explores among other weighty issues the courage needed to mercy kill a loved one – and now he wants to dissect the author's intentions. It would be a challenging discussion with anyone at anytime, let alone a smashed Wamboobi at whatever hour of the morning it was. But he is lucid and funny and wild and I wonder what our neighbors think of all the laughing. When I finally drift back to sleep I have a smile on my face.

The next day is a rest day. Wamboobi is saving himself for a big night, he says, since it's to be our last at Faraway Bay. Mercy, mercy, Mr Percy*.

After dinner and a bit of a jam with the guitars I bail. Wamboobi and his drinking partner – team Martian and Mauritian – look set for a serious session. And I can hear a constant droning coming from the other end of the table. I feel trouble brewing and I don't want to be there when it's cooked.

Many hours later I hear the two of them in the garden outside our window. They're caught in a giggling tangle of ineptitude. One is helping the other up and they're stuck halfway. I'm going to have to go out there or I'll never get back to sleep.

"I am most definitely not drunk," Wamboobi stresses as I pull him upright, "I am merely… enthusiastic."

Mauritania helps me get Wamboobi to the door of our cabin then leaves me to it. I tell Wamboobi I'm putting him to bed but all he does is take one step inside and prop to show me he's still making his own decisions. He no doubt imagines he's frozen like a marble statue but he's teetering more like a clown on a unicycle. I've seen him this way before. There's no point trying to make him do anything so I leave him standing in the dark and go back to bed.

*Tom Waits – Invitation to the Blues

After a time I hear a few halting footsteps and the sound of his body flopping back on his bed, followed by a long sigh. Excellent, I think, soon he will be either asleep or dead and peace will be mine once more.

Not a hope in hell.

"Tonight," comes a voice in the darkness, ". . . I killed the Human Didgeridoo."

"Was that necessary?"

"Absolutely. He was trying to stop me... eating the cherubin."

"Did you?"

"Delicious."

"I'll kill you if you have."

"If you and I..." he says, speaking in weighted, if not altogether measured phrases, "are going on the journey... on The Road, so to speak...then we must learn to eat... everything. Besides, you haven't got it in you."

"To kill you?"

"Correct."

"What makes you think that?"

"Because you are... " long pause, I can almost hear the cognitive malfunction ". . . a numpty."

"Could you kill me?"

"Without a moment's hesitation... I could crush you like a beetle... without remorse... because I have been trained to kill... thirty seven ways... with a paper cup... "

Then he went to sleep. And it's hard to say whether or not my hosts appreciated me bringing my 'producer' along, but I don't think I've ever loved him more than I did at Faraway Bay. Perhaps even enough to kill him.

CLAUDIUS CLAUDIA

I'm not going to bang on about this, but Claude is causing me no end of grief at the moment. Quite apart from the litany of mechanical issues he keeps gifting me, he's also got a chronic, intermittent auto-electrical fault, and there's nothing more evil in a motor vehicle than an intermittent auto-electrical fault. When there's just the two of us he plays merry hell with my head – illuminating the dash with warning lights, overriding the remote and locking me out, fiddling with the house control board – but as soon as I get him to the workshop butter wouldn't melt in the bastard's mouth.

Before I set off on the last, ill-fated leg of the trip* I knew I still had a problem. Naturally he waited till we were at the furthest point away before he showed his hand and cost me five hundred dollars for a flatbed lift home. But at least I now had a recognizable condition to deal with: he'd stopped. And this time he took the house power supply down with him.

At this point I'd like to make it clear I don't begrudge Claude

*To Kakadu and Arnhemland to shoot a Top End travelogue for Tourism Australia.

regular maintenance, indeed I'd already treated him to some splendid new parts from home and abroad and all manner of servicing and reconditioning. And things like renewing springs and shocks I consider par for the course driving on the roads I do, likewise sorting out problems inherited with purchase (no small number, I might add).

But I do baulk at having to replace the same part more than once when we still haven't found the cause of the problem. It invites cruel suggestions from friends, like, "Why don't I buy my alternators in bulk?" and "I should just get a flatbed truck and drive Claude around the country on the back of that." Only my mechanic understands it's no joke: he's grown very wary of even taking my calls of late and rumour has it he's started therapy.

One of my friends in Darwin has a theory that it's karma for all the sponsors' vehicles I've trashed in the past, but that would be cruel justice indeed. I wasn't even driving half of the wrecks I've been blamed for. And since when was television accountable for its actions anyway?

Another of her theories is that Claude is playing up because he's really a Claudia, and what woman wouldn't misbehave if you treated her as a man? But I'm not at all sure I know what this means when applied to *humans*, much less how one sex-differentiates with motor vehicles. Would that mean I should pay more attention to how she looks? Or *feels*, for Christ's sake? No, I think I prefer the straight forward relationship we have going now: I drive him firm but fair, he lets me until he decides not to, I try to patch things up even though I don't always understand, and when he's good and ready we start the cycle again. (Come to think of it there *is* something disturbingly familiar about that pattern.)

Meanwhile I'm no closer to any mechanical explanation for why I keep blowing alternators*, or what the hell the flashing E08 light on the control board means. I thought the gateway on board Mother Theresa was complicated; Claude's got an alien living in the cupboard. And it hates me, too.

But like I said I'm not going to bang on about it. I've got the number of a gun auto-electrician and I'm not afraid to use it. And if all else fails I might even consider a name change.

* For the auto-electrically inclined, apparently a series of unfortunate events had conspired against me, involving a manufacturing fault in a house battery which blew a succession of faulty Chinese-made alternators and eventually killed off the other house battery as well. At the time of publishing all parts were new and authentic and I hadn't had a problem in two whole weeks. Yippee!

WAITING FOR THE GIRL

In the upper reaches of the Adelaide River is an island. On that island lives a man, and a female crocodile called Casey. The man, by admission, is very fond of a drink. The crocodile, by reputation, is very fond of potatoes and gravy. They make an unusual couple.

I first heard of the arrangement while I was selling books at the markets in Darwin. Another couple recently returned from the River recommended I do both the croc jumping tour and the Island visit. It proved good advice.

The Adelaide River is said to have the highest concentration of crocodiles in the world, and it's the undisputed home of the jumping crocodile. Every dry season boatloads of tourists marvel at the agility of these well-conditioned reptiles, capable of propelling more than half their body out of the water to reach a morsel of meat dangled aloft by the tour operators.

Many people disapprove of feeding wild animals to exploit them for commercial gain, but I don't see a whole lot of difference between that and feeding kangaroos at the zoo. Early fears that crocodiles would start humbugging smaller fishing boats for food have not been realized – at least so far – and as one tour operator tells me, it's often the only way many tourists get to see a crocodile at close quarters, even though he doesn't agree with the term "jumping crocodiles".

"They're smart enough to know which boats feed them and which ones don't," he says, " and they exhibit the same traits in the wild: reaching up into trees for birds and snakes, and I've seen them jump up banks to take a pig or a dingo, so it's not as if we're teaching them anything new."

Whatever your stance on the matter it's a captivating spectacle, and another facet in the jewel of the Northern Territory's tourism crown: *Crocodylus porosus.*

Of the three licensed operators who offer croc jumping tours on the Adelaide River I choose the off-broadway operation based at Fogg Dam, not only because it's smaller and more personal than the other two and allows me better videotaping opportunities, but also because they do tours to the island and know how to get in contact with its owner.

The island is about an hour's dinghy ride from the Arnhem

Highway and I arrange to meet my host at the bridge. He's a man in his late fifties with a suntanned face and a pronounced gap between his front teeth, and he warns he's having fuel problems with his outboard motor so the trip may take longer than usual. While I help him load his supplies in the dinghy I give him the abridged story of Claude to put him at ease.

It's a pleasant trip upriver through floodplain country. The mid-morning air is cool against the face and the level terrain is broken by the odd stand of paper bark trees and thicket of bamboo, the silence by the sound of a motor running smoothly and by my host's occasional remarks and ready laugh.

"That bamboo, there," he says at one point, pointing out a stand about three metres in height, "is called *arnhemis**, and it only flowers once every fifty years or so, then dies. When I first bought the island six years ago it'd just been through a flowering cycle and you could barely navigate your way up the river with all the floating bamboo: sticks twenty metres long, some if it." He concludes the commentary with a short burst of his trademark cackle and a slug of beer.

At the island we are met as long lost friends by his pet dog, Hot Dog, the most agreeable fox terrier cross I've encountered in an age. Later Hot Dog shows me his party trick and sings, wailing like a canine Chad Morgan** to his master's unmusical mouth organ, but for now we follow his wagging tail up the pontoon's walkway

* Strictly speaking it's Arnhem Land Bamboo or *Bambusa arnhemica*.

** Legendary Australian country/comic performer also known as The Sheik of Scrubby Creek who built a career on a great set of teeth and a swag of songs with amusing lyrics and bizarre noises.

THE MOTORS

Above: *Mother Theresa Bogged, Blackall, QLD* (story page 36).

Below: *Claude at Rest, Victoria River, NT* (story page 132).

THE LIFESTYLES

Above: *Good Grass, Yorke Peninsula, SA* (story page 73).
Below: *Cambodian Comfort, Port Roper, NT* (story page 151).

THE PROVOCATIVE

Above: *Bradshaw Woman, North Kimberley, WA* (story page 134).

Below: *Artists or Vandals? Cape York, QLD.*

THE AIRBORNE
Above: *Flying Lizard, Coolibah Station, NT* (story page 133).
Below: *The Undeserving Claude, Cairns, QLD*.

THE DECORATED

Above: *The Bottle (& sex toy) Tree, Eyre Hwy, Nullarbor Plain.*

Below: *The Shoe Tree, Eyre Hwy, Nullarbor Plain.*

THE HEADLESS

Above: *We're Out of Here, Karratha Salt Mines, WA.*

Below: *Croc Shock, Wyndham, WA* (story page 53).

THE WARNINGS

Above: *Strange Fruit, Central QLD.*

Below: *Chicken Mining, Coen, Cape York, QLD* (story page 202).

DIP
THERIA

DOUBLE
DIP-
PING

SKINNY
DIP

NO
SHOOTING
ON TOWN
COMMON

CHILL OUT
NOT FLAT OUT
AFTER
BEFORE

to the leafy compound. The focal point of the island seems to be *Casey's Bar,* a small dining room built in underneath some private quarters. A large open deck connecting a semi-detached wing of rooms makes up the rest of the accommodation complex, while a few outbuildings and an old barge tethered to the riverbank are the remaining signs of habitation.

"On shopping days I like to relax with a few beers once I've unpacked the boat," he tells me, cracking another can. "Sort of like a treat." He continues treating himself throughout the afternoon and evening as I learn his story.

He tells me he bought the island at the behest of his wife of twenty years, but she couldn't tolerate his drinking and left him to it.

"She was smarter than me. She didn't think it was a good idea for me to be a publican."

"We're still best of friends," he stresses. "But she's as stubborn as they come. I've told her if I can handle her stubbornness then she can handle my drinking, but she won't have it."

Now she lives in town and he lives alone on the island, running the modest bar-come-B&B single-handedly. He's had mates help out from time to time but he prefers to be on his own if he's not with a woman. He's tried Internet dating a couple of times but without success.

"I've had two cups of coffee with two women, and that's it. So now it's just Casey and me. And the dog, of course, but he's a boy. "

Casey the crocodile first started getting fed by the previous owner, who discovered she had a predilection for scraps, especially potatoes and gravy. At that stage she used to come right up into the bar for a feed, but that tended to make the clients anxious so a more safety-conscious routine was developed.

Now she has her own feeding station about halfway up the hill so the guests can watch from the balcony above. He also recently installed a fence between him and her dinner plate after Casey decided she wanted a piece of him for dessert one night.

"Yeah, she had a go at me a couple of times and I had to give her a clout with the frying pan." He shows me the sizeable dint her nose made in the pan. "Now I keep the fence between us, although she does show a bit more respect when I lift the pan.

"When I first started in tourism I went to a seminar and the speaker said, 'If you've got a remote operation it's better to be different than better.' But I don't want a public liability case sending me broke so the difference has to be safe."

In the afternoon I rig up some extra spotlights around the feeding station so I have enough light to video Casey from the balcony. My host takes a couple of shrimp from his permanent trap and we do a spot of fishing to pass the time. We catch only catfish, but it's mesmerising to watch the brown water eddy and swirl as it carries logs and rafts of debris upstream, reminding me of books I've read that were set on the great rivers of America. There's something both soothing and menacing at the same time about a river that shows you only its surface. As darkness falls I test the spotlights for coverage and settle in to wait.

"I can't promise she'll come, of course," my host says. "She is a woman after all, and it's mating season and she might have gone off already. But usually I'll see the big males cruising up and down the river before that happens. Normally they swim low in the water and you don't see much more than the eyes and a bow wave, but when they're cruising for a mate they sit up high in the water."

Over dinner, the conversation gets back to around to women – as if it ever ventures too far from it when males are alone – and he tells me he'd like to find someone to share the island with.

"It needs two people, this place. And I miss their company. It's what everyone wants, isn't it, someone to share their life with?"

He grins across the table at me and I notice he's starting to look the worse for wear from all the beers he's put away. He hasn't lost his sense of humour but there's a sadness leaking into his boat as he sinks lower in the water. I try to change tack and bring the subject back to Casey with only partial success.

"I'm ninety percent certain she'll come up tonight, but she is a wild animal and she is a woman, so who can say?"

He cackles again and it occurs to me how often he makes reference to her sex, indeed how everything seems to be classified according to its sex. Hot Dog is good company "but he's a boy", Casey will only eat fish if it's cooked because "she's a woman and she's fussy as." Is this what it boils down to when men live without women? And what's at the core of the role-playing in men's prisons? If a man is denied female company does he naturally divide what's available into a tolerable masculine-feminine ratio?

Once we are fed he cooks Casey's dinner – lightly fried fish, leftover caramelized potatoes, a tomato, lettuce – and takes it to her station, calling her tenderly, "Come on beautiful. Here's your dinner, lovely Tarpon and spuds and salad, everything you like."

Then he empties the pan onto her plate and bangs it hard against the aluminium tray several times to alert her that dinner is served.

We relocate to the balcony above and I play him a few 'love done me wrong' songs. He reciprocates with an unaccompanied version of Rocky Mountain High, the complete lyrics to which he notably recalls. It proves to be his swansong and shortly thereafter he excuses himself and retires, listing badly and sitting very low in the water. His parting words are, "I'm still fifty-fifty sure Casey'll come up," and then he seems to remember something important and says, "my wife was…" but the thought sinks before it's unloaded and he pulls out.

For the next two hours I wait with fading expectation. Every fifteen minutes or so I shine the torch down to the water and up the path she has worn to her plate, hoping to catch the crocodile's red eyes in the beam. But the only interest I see in Casey's dinner is from a cane toad, hooking into a free meal. I recall a conversation we had earlier in the evening about the increasing incidence of crocodiles being poisoned from eating cane toads and wonder what would happen if Casey found one on her dinner plate. To satisfy my curiosity I walk down to her station and the toad hops away*.

I needn't have worried. She doesn't come before I go to bed, or indeed anytime during the night, and in the morning the crows and the kites eat her dinner; all except the lettuce.

"The only explanation is she's already mating," is my host's shrugging explanation as he prepares to run me back to the highway.

* See photo, colour section one, page 5, bottom.

We make the long trip back downriver with the outboard motor refusing to run properly and the dinghy sitting very low in the water.

TAK MAN

My new friend has a tax problem. Only he's from Cambodia so he pronounces it *tak*. It must be worrying him because he tells me about it within minutes of meeting. I think he imagines I can help him.

I'd wandered into Port Roper just to see what I could see, and because I heard about a fisherman who'd been living there forever and thought he'd be a good man to meet. He was, but he wasn't in the mood for doing anything for the camera. All in the line of duty he'd recently been knocked unconscious by an unidentified flying fish, spiked through the thumbnail by a grunter (Javelin Fish) and sidelined by an arthritic wrist. To say he wasn't having a good run would be noise pollution. He directed me towards the crabbers' camp a few kilometres further downriver.

"They're good value, the boys," he said. "They'll give you a story."

There isn't so much a town at Port Roper but a handful of demountables and sheds mostly owned by the fisherman, and a boat ramp. In the middle of the dry season you might also see a wishlot of amateur fishermen camped along the foreshore, interstaters who make the trip hoping to catch a monster barramundi, but late in the season as it was I met only one camp of diehards from the Sunshine Coast in Queensland. The Roper is about half a kilometre wide at that point, mangrove-lined and muddy, and the terrain is tidal mudflat and grey sand. Add the heat and the midges to the picture and it's no place to be unless you have good reason.

The reason the crabbers are there is logical enough, but another reason occurred to me as I drove within sight of their camp. Many of the crabbers in the western Gulf of Carpentaria are Vietnamese and in some ways the place must remind them of home. The climate, the big water, the geographical similarities with the Mekong Delta, for instance, must offer some comfort. And perhaps these were men who yearned for the days of old back in the home country, when a decent living could still be made in those heavily fished and polluted river systems of south east Asia.

Certainly their camp looked much like the fishing villages I've seen in Vietnam. Whether solely for reasons of practicality or partly by native inclination the half dozen or so shacks that made up the camp were all built on stilts out over the water, so they had level access from one door and their dinghies moored at the other.

Most were constructed of used corrugated iron and scrub timber and several had brightly coloured plastic sheeting or bits of tarpaulin for walls. One even had an old caravan with its wheels raised half a metre above the ground annexed to the main building, suggesting the river shipped its banks during the wet season. The overall effect was one of enduring impermanence.

Further south I heard of Vietnamese crabbers literally living in the trees on planks of timber and whatever else they could scrounge, so I guess this community was upmarket by comparison.

It was early afternoon when I arrived and there was no sign of life. Assuming they were either out checking their pots or sleeping I retreated to do some work. When I returned several hours later there was a friendly wave offered from the shack furthest from where I'd parked so I wandered on down.

The wave belonged to a Cambodian man who owned a smile to match and he invited me inside to join him and his offsider for a beer*. His offsider was younger than him by about twenty years and just a hospitable, and between them they agreed it would be no problem to take me out crabbing the next morning, especially once I told them the segment would probably be aired in Cambodia. (To be honest I wasn't sure of this, but I knew Vietnam was a core market for Australia Network and figured it was a safe bet.)

And so it was sitting on an upturned crab basket drinking warm Heinekin as the sun set on another hot Gulf afternoon, that I learned how a humble crab fisherman could earn himself a *tak pwobwem.*

"My before boss I say to him you *fik* my *tak* so I no worry," he tells me, "but he no do and now the girl tell me I need pay *deventy doudan doddar* in *dik munt*."

He's no orator, my new friend, but his message is clear. He trusted his previous boss to sort out his tax but either it wasn't done or he didn't understand what he had to do and now the accountant is insisting the taxman wants seventy grand in six months.

* See photo, colour section two, page 2, bottom.

"I pay, no worry," he assures me. "I pay already *dwo doudan* every month, but they no want. And how I find *deventy doudan doddar* out here?" He gestures in a sweep at his slapstick humpy thrown together after his previous one was levelled by the last cyclone, at the scattering of ropes and corks and pots and fuel drums, at the putrid pile of bait gone off since the freezer broke down, at the river and the mangroves and the mud, the mud, the beautiful stinking mud.

Mud crabs in the Gulf are big business and setups like this are not uncommon. The land is usually leased from the Aborigines or the Crown by entrepreneurial souls who effectively employ the fishermen to supply them with crabs. On a regular basis they bring supplies and equipment in and take away a backload of crabs for market. Consequently the fishermen rely heavily on their boss, especially if their grasp of the language is poor.

My new friend tells me in one good year he earned over three hundred thousand dollars crabbing, and on the current markets rate of around four hundred dollars a basket it's not hard to top a hundred grand in an average year. With figures like that it's just as easy to imagine how a tax problem could develop, and to sympathise with a simple fisherman with no concept of things like provisional tax and BAS and PAYG.

We set off into a pink dawn to run the pots and the first one is lifted before the sun breaks the rim. Half a dozen crabs are tipped scuttling and squirting into the holding bin. As quickly as they go in they are tied with string to keep their strong jaws from latching onto anything fleshy, like a careless finger or a bare foot. And as quickly as one lot is tied the contents of another trap are emptied into the bin. It's repetitive work.

Occasionally a catfish caught in a pot will break the monotony, or a trap will surface crushed and empty and the boys will speculate whether it was a shark or a stingray responsible – everything loves a free feed of crabs – but mostly the pattern is unchanged: lift, empty, re-bait, throw back, then drive to the next trap for the younger man, and catch, test for fullness and size and either toss overboard or tie for the elder.

Unlike most states, in the Northern Territory it's legal to take Jennies (females), unless they're carrying eggs, or "in berry" as the term goes. It's an issue that evokes strong opinions both ways. While the short-term benefit of leaving the breeders in the water seems irrefutable, states that follow this practice are seeing a disturbing sex-imbalance develop in their stocks, and there is a school of thought that suggests the long-term disadvantages may outweigh the advantages. In any case the NT seems to have circumvented the problem by keeping license numbers very low.

While they work I shoot video and attempt to interview them, perchance to get a few insights into the philosophy of fishing, but the younger man is still developing his, and the older man is too pre-occupied.

The young man likes being out on the water because "there's no-one around to humbug you" and no boss to resent. About the only thing he misses are the girls. He doesn't mind the crocodiles but the sharks scare him – "some of them as big as the boat, five, six metres" – and he still loves eating crabs because, I get the impression, he wouldn't be able to afford them if he was back in Darwin. "Expensive stuff," he tells me.

The older man doesn't like crabs much – "I see every day I no want to eat" – and he's still got *tak* issues, even out in the Gulf on a beautiful clear morning. It's eating him up. He's even calculated how many days he'd have to stay in goal to pay off the debt if it comes to that. He's seriously concerned his lifestyle is going to be taken away from him if he can't come up with the money.

"I no want to owe anything. I pay, I pay, little bit at time," he tells me with a faint pleading edge to his words, as if the little story I'm doing will paint him in a good light and sway the ATO.

In-between his plea-bargaining he offers snippets of his life story. He escaped the constraints of growing up in a rich family by walking away to live his own life. Then he endured extreme poverty for years, refusing to fall back on his heritage, before he found his feet. He even survived Pol Pot and the Khmer Rouge by running away to Thailand to become a jeweller. Now it looks like the Australian Tax Office has got the better of him. It's almost a crime, a tax crime, indeed.

We catch about two and a half baskets of crabs and my host insists I stay and share a meal with them when we return. He cooks crab in black bean and chili sauce, and stir-fried beef. It's delicious. Again there is warm Heinekin to wash it down.

When I leave I know they will have a short sleep, then get up in the afternoon to mend the broken pots and attend to any other repairs, and maybe do a bit more work on the house before the evening meal. Then they will sleep and rise and do it all over again: cut the bait, empty the pots, tie the crabs, pack the baskets, pay the *tak*, pay the *tak*, pay the *tak*…

"Australia good country, I like very much."

"Why?" I ask him.

"In Australia no-one die from no food. In Australia nobody go hungry.

"Just too many *tak*. I catch crab pay *tak*. My boss take crab for sell he pay *tak*. Restaurant buy for cook he pay *tak*. Too many *tak*."

We hear you, brother. We hear you.

FIRE

We *were* all planning to head off early for a day at the beach and a spot of bull-catching, but a last-minute decision to make a few repairs on the Toyota before we left probably saved the farm from burning down. That gave the fire time to show its hand and us reason to change our plans. When I amble up from my camp on the river, wondering what happened to the early start, the sky behind the house is a billowing curtain of menace and a dozen or more people stand watching.

With approaching danger there is usually an obvious moment of awareness when spectators become participants and the tempo changes. At that point actions become either more purposeful or more erratic. Fires often incite the latter, but in this instance it was very much the former. Even when my host casually says to me, "Sorry, we're in panic mode around here," I'm reminded of an old Thai man I knew who used to say, "Make haste slowly."

There is no screaming "Fire!" or running about yelling orders, just a dozen or so men walking around making preparations to defend their livelihood from a bushfire no more than a few kilometres distant. Empty forty-four gallon drums are loaded onto trucks for filling with water, spot fires are lit in the scrub around the machinery sheds to back burn before the main front arrives, a truck with a load of hay is moved into the open and branches of trees are broken for fire switches. Few words are exchanged and yet there seems to be an order, a chain of command, with everyone knowing exactly what he is meant to do.

I have the camera with me and I ask the boss what he wants me to do, shoot or help. He grins and said, "Both", and gives me the job of filling the water drums so I could video the action and still be useful. From there I can also see several women sat by the demountables watching their men, the fire, the sky; a study in anxious calm.

From my vantage on the tray back of the ute I also notice a fuel tank and a stack of drums that seem perilously positioned. The fire is approaching from the southeast through lightly timbered coolibah and ironwood country that hasn't been burnt for a few years and it's loving the dry fuel. If it gets into that wet fuel we'll all go up.

The water drums filled I deliver the makeshift fire truck to the boys and they slip into a routine as readily as if they rehearsed this every day: a drum goes over on its side, water gushes from the hole, buckets catch the flow, carriers douse the flames, repeat as necessary till either supply or job is done. Again they work with the minimum of fuss, as if the urgency of the situation doesn't allow room for ego, won't tolerate the waste of energy. Human

Resource departments looking for fresh teambuilding exercises could do worse than send their staff off to fight fires.

I go for a walk with the camera towards the fire looking for the boss. The front is too hot for me to get close, but walking along the dirt track towards it I notice hundreds of insects scuttling from one side to the other. The fire is still too far away for even me to be sure which side of the track is burning, yet they are escaping to the right side. How do they know?

I catch the boss walking back from the front and he tells me the front is doing about thirty kilometres an hour and heading our way. He's worried about getting enough back burning done before it arrives.

"One of those jobs we know we should do every year," he says, "and we were aware it needed doing, but somehow it got put off the agenda." He shrugs and turns back to what is now very much on the agenda.

"How much gear do you have in the sheds?"

"A bit. Maybe better it burns and I get the insurance," he laughs.

I tell him my concerns for the fuel dump but he doesn't say much in reply. He seems more interested in why the beetles know which side of the road they should be on. Then a cry goes up from the sheds and he quickens his pace into something approaching a jog, one of the rare times I see anyone break out of a walk.

The alarm is for an outbreak beside one of the sheds. It's all hands on deck and even the boss's grandsons – plucky boys of eight or ten years – are working switches on the flames now climbing up the dry grass and licking the bark of the scrub trees. One of the boys turns from the fire and puts his hands to his stinging eyes and I'm too proud of him to remember to video the moment.

The other men are ringers and roustabouts normally employed to run cattle, cook meals and tend station duties. Now they are fire fighters. A few are WWOOFers* from Europe, getting a real taste of life on an Australian farm. They will experience few things in Australia more real than a summer bushfire.

We bring the outbreak to heel but at the frontline the flames dance through the scrub like they're happy to be free, touching the grass here, exploding the undergrowth there, slithering up a trunk to torch the leaves of a tree before leaping across to the next, and the next. And in their wake they leave only a wasteland of spot fires, smoke and soot, a blackened forest of naked trees that stretches on forever.

But it's the noise you remember most, the roar that drowns out speech and steals the oxygen from the air, literally sucking it from your lungs. That's why grown men cry, that's why they turn their backs on the fight. They would carry on blind if they had to, but they can't fight when they can't breathe. It's a formidable foe.

And it won't lie down. Just when we get the first outbreak under control another flares up and threatens to engulf the sheds again. This time we have no water because the boys have taken the "fire engine" down to the cattle yards where fifty head of cleanskin bulls are also under threat. This time there is only the boss and I.

And the fuel dump, right beside the shed.

*Willing Workers On Organic Farms.

It's one of those moments where a journalist has to decide whether to help or shoot. I try to do both with limited success. The locked-off* shots I get are only average and the fire gets away from us. I'm consoled the fire is too hungry, too keen, and would've beaten two men with branches anyway.

This time I tell the boss I'm terrified about the fuel dump but he tells me it'll be fine. I admire his calm but I really don't share it. Half of me wants to stay and fight and half wants to run. Luckily help arrives before I have to make the choice. We contain the blaze and let it burn a break around the shed and the fuel dump. I'm still uneasy as I work hard to keep the flames from the vicinity of the drums.

Later I learn there was no fuel in the drums anyway, it was a disused dump. In the height of the action the boss was having a loan of me. When I finally twig he just laughs.

"Yeah, we knew it wouldn't go bang," he said.

Meanwhile, down at the cattle yards the fire is circling the fence. The bulls are safe – and surprisingly calm – but if it burns the timber rails they will escape. The boys are emptying buckets of water on the most threatening breaks and beating the smaller flames down with switches, but the worst is over now.

I speak with one of the ringers at the yards, a tall, quietly-spoken man who's so black I can't see his face in the shadow under his hat.

"Do you reckon we've got it beat?"

*Camera mounted on the tripod and framed up to one field of vision.

"Yeah," he answers, looking away from the camera so now I can barely hear him as well as hardly see him, "It's gone down to the river where it'll probably burn itself out." He indicates the direction of the river then looks back to camera.

"Just lucky the house didn't catch on fire or anything, or any of the cars."

And only then do I remember Claude. I've left him to fend for himself on the banks of the river. I run down not knowing what I'll find, but he's sitting there safe as a mortgage, smoke billowing up around him with kites and ibises soaring high above. Remembering the boss's crack about insurance I'm only half-pleased.

Back at the scene the boss is tending spot fires with the Dutch WWOOFer, watering the smoldering logs and hidden embers likely to re-ignite.

"That was a close one," he says. "Lucky we didn't go bullcatching early, eh?"

The young man from Holland has worked tirelessly and now surveys the scene. All around the homestead and outbuildings is black and empty, no grass, no scrub, not a tinge of green. The only visible signs of life are the ibises now coming down to pick through the ashen waste for roasted insects and grilled lizards.

"You won't be needing to burn back now, yes?" he says, mopping his brow.

"No, she'll be right this year," says the boss, keen eyes picking out another threat. "Just watch that toilet over there don't burn down, would you?" I guess he'd hate to lose the dunny now after working so hard to save the castle.

Later over a cup of tea the boss tells me he's had worse fires on the property.

"We lost a few horses, one time. Got trapped in the corner of the paddock. Had nowhere to go so they run back through the fire."

"Do you think we manage fire well in this country?"

"No, we don't. You saw a good example why this morning. We should burn off more. National Parks included. National Parks are the worst."

At that point I hear that unmistakable crackling sound again and look around for something else about to flare up. But it's only the campfire renewing its vows. The boss laughs at my twitchiness. He's a cooler man than I.

IRON COWBOY

I couldn't say what speed we were doing except that it was breakneck. Tree trunks barely missed us on both sides, overhanging branches threatened to knock our heads off and unseen potholes tried to pitch us from the rig. At times I couldn't see any sort of path through the scrub never mind the bulls we were chasing. Then suddenly we'd be out on the plains again and flying, the quarry a-scatter in the distance and any benefit from the flatter ground offset by the increased speed. Hanging on with two hands would have been chore enough; trying to manage with one *and* keep the camera on the action was downright heroic, I decided.

Then I looked down and noticed the two kids calmly eating fruit from a tin, the littlest one with a spoon, if you please.

Bull catching in a cut-down 4x4 is exhilarating stuff, no question. On the thrill scale I'd put it somewhere between a wild carnival ride and being a passenger in a rally car, only there's no safety harness and the competition is more unpredictable. Yet according to my driver fast is the only way to go.

"Yeah, when you're pokin' back off 'em they gallop, gallop, gallop for miles, some of 'em do," he says. "But if you get into 'em and up 'em quick you blow the gas out of 'em, yeah."

Indeed a couple of times I saw the bullocks run out of puff and fall over even before the rig touched them. But just because they're out of puff doesn't mean they're out of fight. These bulls are wild animals and they don't always like being run down by a noisy big horse with rubber tyres strapped to its front bumper.

"Do they ever turn the tables on you?" I ask.

"The big ones will," he says. "Not so much these young mickeys we were chasing today, but when them big fellas really want to have a go at you they'll come back and push you around a bit, yeah."

Which is an exciting prospect, especially when you consider the next stage in the process where the cowboy has to jump from the rig and toss the beast on its side. With his bare hands!

This calls for a show of equal parts comedy and finesse, with the thrower running alongside the bullock and giving its tail a twist and a wrench and presto, the animal is flipped over ready for hobbling. I watched this several times and I don't imagine it's as easy as it looks, and it didn't look that easy. To begin with even the "mickeys" don't seem to appreciate having their tails yanked and often turn around and have a go. I can only imagine "them big fellas" would be even less pleased.

There are other bull catching rigs set up with mechanical arms on the side, but I liked the organic nature of this hands-on method, and especially the tail-throwing spectacle, which is the best part. Unless the bull gets up and tries to toss the rig, of course, which I imagine would be pretty entertaining stuff, especially if you're in it at the time.

"Do you think it'd work as a tourist attraction?" the property's owner asks me later.

"Providing you've got enough public liability insurance," I say.

"We're thinking of doing that: the bull catching," he continues in all seriousness.

His property is located on the Northern Territory side of the Gulf of Carpentaria, and the owner tells me his son, my driver, is the best bull catcher he's ever seen.

"His grandfather was good; I saw him ride his horse up between two bullocks, grab their tails and throw both at the same time, then keep on riding. And I was handy enough in my time. But this kid's in another class. What you saw him do today he can do at night with nothing but a spotlight."

Now there's a tourist attraction with bragging rights.

The subject of tourism has come up because it's a pertinent issue in the bush these days. A lot of property owners are looking at ways to supplement their incomes by tapping into the burgeoning tourist market. And while tourism on working cattle stations has been around a while, travellers are always eager for fresh locations and new experiences. The owner here thinks he might have both, and I suspect he's right.

The property is called Seven Emu Station and stretches between two major Gulf Rivers, the Robinson and the Calvert, containing some of the most spectacular gorge country I've seen. In addition it has a long stretch of coastline with real sand – a rarity in the Southern Gulf country – and a wide range of terrain from tidal flats and coastal heath to paperbark swamps, open woodlands of bloodwood, ironwood and snappy gum eucalypts, and spinifex and grass plains between the scrub lines.

The fishing is excellent thanks to negligible impact from tourism over the years, and the property is rich in history, with the explorer Ludwig Leichhardt passing through in the mid-eighteen hundreds on his first expedition from south east Queensland to the Top End of the Territory. According to his journal, on that journey he killed and ate seven young emus in the vicinity of what he subsequently named Seven Emu Creek, and the property takes its name from the same event.

Till now the station has limited the access to camping permits for a small number of loyal campers from all over Australia – while I was camped at the Robinson River crossing I spoke with several people who'd been coming for over twenty years – but now the family is considering low impact facilities along several of the more picturesque gorges.

"My father always told me to hang on to the property and don't change it," the owner tells me. "One day Australians will want to see their country natural, the way it always was; natural."

He though his father was crazy to have such ideas at the time, but forty years later it's clear he showed remarkable foresight about an industry that was barely born.

He tells me his father also used to hunt crocodiles in the swamps on the property using rafts he made from pandanus and paperbark, and recalls as a young boy having to light and tend fires around billabongs to stop the crocodiles escaping to another billabong overnight. Exciting stuff, no doubt, but I daresay an unlikely tourism opportunity. The bull catching, on the other hand, I think could be a winner.

Of course it's common practice on stations to muster the cleanskin cattle, and however that can be done effectively – by helicopter, horseback or bullcatcher – is a good method from a station perspective. This one just happens to have the added bonus of being passenger-friendly, so why not share the experience with the thrill-hungry public?

"You've got bungy jumping, jumping out of planes," the owner justifies, "bull catching is no different; a bit more safer I'd reckon.

"And it's good for kids, young kids you wouldn't see bungy jumping or sky diving… and the thrill of chasing a wild bull; that's an excitement on its own."

It's hard to argue. There was no shortage of thrills with my ride, and apart from having my hat knocked off my head by a low-slung branch there were no spills. Indeed it was very much a family affair with mum and the two kids, as I said earlier, comfortable enough to eat snacks. In fact to hear my driver talk you'd think it was no more than a pleasant Sunday drive in the country, in spite of my assertions to the contrary.

"You've got to keep your eyes on the bullock and your eyes on the trees overhead and your eyes on the track; you've got to have four eyes!" I say.

"Yeah," he laughs modestly, "I just try and keep an eye on things and hope for the best, really."

MORNING GLORY

Driving through the Gulf Country was prettier than expected, especially on the Northern Territory side. Instead of the relatively flat terrain of the eastern Gulf – which I'd travelled before – the west is predominantly stone country, shaped almost mountainous in parts with vast slopes of timber and picturesque river crossings.

The road forms part of the Savannah Way from Cairns to Broome and sees plenty of traffic during the winter months, but once the weather starts to warm up the Grey Nomads head south and normal levels of inactivity return. I did the trip in early October and didn't pass more than a dozen cars between Borroloola and Burketown.

In Burketown, though, there were signs of life, only not as I knew it. The caravan park was mostly full and parked outside on the street were several, large cigar-shaped trailers the like of which I'd never seen before. They belonged, I soon discovered, to an eclectic knit of travellers who called themselves morning glory hunters.

I'd noticed the 'Welcome to Morning Glory Country' sign as I crossed the border into Queensland but took scant notice. Everywhere had its little boast and if they thought the land brought out the best in their men, why not? And it was with this idle thought in mind that I encountered my first glory hunters.

They were an unassuming couple sitting at the caravan park café waiting for their order. He was middle aged with a ruddy complexion and snowy hair. She looked younger and could still be called pretty. And when she said they were there for the morning glory I wasn't quite sure how to respond.

Over the next few days I came to realize the sexual innuendo was all part of the deal, and they each had their stories of friends and family being overheard ringing to ask if they got a good morning glory that day. But what they were really referring to was a meteorological phenomenon that happens only in the Gulf of Carpentaria.

Because of the region's unique topography, at certain times of the year long waves of roll-shaped clouds develop off western Cape York and travel across the Gulf, before disintegrating overland somewhere southwest of Burketown. The waves usually form overnight and reach Burketown by morning, making it the most logical place to see them, and therefore to ride them.

The pilots fly self-launching gliders they tow disassembled in the long trailers I'd seen when I arrived. Many drive for days to get there and most I spoke to were repeat offenders.

"It's the ultimate ride for a glider pilot," one experienced morning glory hunter told me. "It's just so smooth, like the cloud's been carved with a butter knife, and the lift is so reliable you can glide for hundreds of kilometres without turning the engine on."

To be honest I'd heard about roll clouds back in my days as a weatherman but I'd forgotten the colloquial name. Now my interest was piqued again. And since I was planning to prop in Burketown while I organized a trip to Sweers Island for the Tourism clip, I decided to follow the story.

So the next morning saw me stumbling to the airport in total darkness with the original couple I'd met at the café, hoping conditions were suitable for a morning glory. The air was dry and warm and my companions were very guarded in assessing our chances. I learned this was par for the course for glory hunters. The waves don't happen every day and I guess after a few wrong calls they learn to hedge their bets. They reminded me very much of meteorologists.

But once we reached the airport and began prepping the aircraft the general consensus was that there wasn't enough moisture in the air for a wave that morning.

"When we *are* going to get a wave we spend a lot of time wiping dew from the wings, while we wait for enough light to take off," I'm told. "This morning, nothing. We'll hang around, anyway, because you never know. But it doesn't look likely."

So we waited, just in case, but the consensus opinion proved correct. There was no wave, and eight o'clock saw us returning to camp to wait another day.

"Sometimes you have to wait a week or more for a wave," one pilot told me. "And sometimes you get lucky and get one straight off."

Throughout the course of that day I learned just how much of a big thing this roll cloud was. Not only was I sharing the story with several other camera crews – one from Britain, one from Japan – but there was also a visiting academic from Massachusetts, USA, there especially to study the morning glory.

"Cape York provides the perfect setting for these waves to form," the professor tells me, "because it generates sea breezes coming from the east and the west which meet over the peninsula and trigger the waves, which then travel across the Gulf of Carpentaria drawing up the moist air that condenses to form the cloud.

"And that's what is particular to this region: the fact that as the moisture is drawn up it forms a cloud, so you can see it. In other parts of the world these waves are believed to be happening far more regularly than we see the morning glory, but you just can't see them."

On the second morning everything was different. To begin with we felt the wind from the leading cloud passing overhead before we reached the airport. And there was dew on the planes, litres of it, and there was much wiping up and wringing out while we waited for the sun to rise. This time there was no question we'd get a morning glory.

To shoot some air-to-air vision I'd pre-arranged a lift in a beautifully restored aircraft called an Auster, a small, fun, British-made single engine aircraft. We set off after the gliders and initially flew 'upstream', in the wrong direction. Visibility was poor and the waves we saw didn't seem to fit the "carved with a knife" image I had in my mind's eye. We turned around and chased the lead wave.

When we found it there was no confusion. The primary wave looked like a never-ending roll of cotton wool suspended in thin air, except the edges were sharp and clear. Even where an occasional tuft of cloud protruded from the roll the definition was high, in spite of a sky that was more grey than blue. Only the leading edge closest to the ground was fragmented where the updraft met the moist roll, as if a giant comb had teased out the wisps of cloud to make a very happening fringe. I resent the way the word "awesome" has been hijacked by people who think a good latte warrants the term, but this was a truly awesome sight.

As we soared over the barrel of the wave my pilot pointed to the altimetre on the instrument panel, indicating the rising needle. Then he looked at me and smiled.

"We were getting enough lift to glide in front of the wave *almost* without engine power," he told me later, "but for a powered aircraft, pretty good."

The gliders, of course, had no need of their motors, and when we caught up with my original couple the first thing I noticed as they surfed along the wave was their stilled propeller.

"When you first contact the cloud," he'd told me the day before, "you normally don't come from above, you come in at the cloud, and when you feel the lift you shut down the engine and away you go.

"Typically, at six hundred feet we're looking for a place to land, not shutting down the engine, but the lift is so strong that once you're on it you know you're going somewhere.

"It's exhilarating, a different kind of adrenaline rush. It's the power of nature and what she can produce for us, and how we can enjoy it without harming anything.

"And the fact that it only happens regularly in Burketown, Australia, and even then not every day, makes it pretty special."

Footnote. By the way, when I arrived in Burketown I had an air conditioner problem and the unit was rattling slightly, a noise that was quickly drawn to my attention by my fellow residents in the caravan park. That it hadn't been picked up before then shouldn't have surprised me; these were glider pilots, after all, accustomed to taking their air in silence. I had it attended to in Cairns lest I met them again.

MOTHER RAINFOREST

The first thing I notice about the woman is that she seems to have three breasts. But because I'm in a hurry to get the camera out and start shooting I don't give it more than a passing thought. Then by the time I work out what's happening I realise how appropriate the observation is anyway.

Her name is Margit and she's an ex-zookeeper turned injured wildlife carer on the Atherton Tablelands, and she has a Lumholtz Tree Kangaroo that comes to visit her from the rainforest. That's why I've rushed to get there and set up the camera gear, because she's rung to tell me Geoffrey the tree kangaroo is sitting outside on a branch ready to come into her house. I need the shot of him coming in from the forest or it will look like he's a tame animal.

Prior to meeting Margit I'd always thought animal carers were bleeding hearts latching onto a furry cause, but this woman is as pragmatic as a soldier. When she eventually reveals her third breast to me – an infant Agile Wallaby she's had down her blouse for comfort and warmth – she suggests mine is a common misconception.

"People often think I do this because old ladies need this sort of thing, but I believe the contact is important for these animals. I usually get them when their mothers have been road killed or dog killed – it's about fifty-fifty – and aside from their injuries they're often very sad when they come in.

"Most people think the newborns are the hardest to look after, but they haven't developed the bond of a three- or four-month-old. Some of them just want to die."

She's under no illusions about why they come back out of the rainforest to visit. "They come for the easy feed, not for me. I don't encourage dependency. As soon as I can teach them the skills they need to survive they return to the forest."

Which is another part of the story I'd never really considered before; that orphaned animals have to be taught everything, even how to climb trees!

"I don't physically climb the trees myself to show them, but I do introduce them to climbing on the smaller, isolated trees like their mothers would, or trees with lots of undergrowth to break their falls. And I teach them which leaves they can eat and which are poisonous. There's a lot to learn if you're an infant tree kangaroo."

The house is like an animal hospital. There's a fledgling bird of prey in a box of straw in the pantry, the young Agile Wallaby hangs in a bag on the doorknob (when it's not around the zookeepers neck) and any number of cheeky Paddy Melon Wallabies that come and go as they please. There's also a lovable, blind tree kangaroo that hops around the house and manages to avoid most of the furniture.

Most of these animals have been brought to the zookeeper to nurse back to health. The young raptor will get a visit from the vet the next day to determine whether its wing will need to be amputated, the wallabies were road accident casualties delivered by concerned passers-by (those that haven't wandered in for the free handout), and a vet in Cairns is making up some optic lenses for the tree kangaroo. I grew up on a farm with a 'survival of the fittest' approach to animals, but when you see this side of the story it's hard not to be impressed by the extent of care, and how many people offer their time and expertise free of charge.

But it's Geoffrey that's the star turn of this hospital.

"He's a wild animal so I can't guarantee when he'll come in," Margit told me when I first contacted her. "But I'll ring you if he does."

When the call came I was about twenty minutes from the Lodge and the zookeeper wasn't sure Goeffrey would stay sitting in the tree till we arrive.

"He's there now and I'm ignoring him, but he might jump down and come inside anyway. If you hurry he might still be there."

We did and he was, large as life, Geoffery the tree kangaroo – orphaned as a joey, raised by the zookeeper, now lord of his patch and frequent visitor to his old home – sitting on a low branch outside the lodge waiting to come in for a feed.

If you've never seen a tree kangaroo they are rather lumpier than you might imagine, especially to be climbing around in trees. The head is smallish by comparison and blunted like that of a wombat or a possum, the body is round and heavy-based and the tail is long and somewhat lifeless. It's about the least agile-looking tree animal I've ever seen.

"The tail lost its prehensile abilities when it evolved, so it can't wrap it around branches like a possum," Margit tells me. "And it doesn't need the strength of a terrestrial kangaroo's. They use it mainly for balance."

But what they lack in agility they make up for in strength and the limbs are powerful, suited for leaping and gripping, a prime example of which happens when Geoffery springs from his limb onto the back of the zookeeper to be taken inside for his meal. It's one of those crossover moments between man and nature that never fails to delight.

While Margit prepares sweet potato wedges and fresh green salad for Geoffrey's main course he snacks on a compote of cashew nuts*, looking entirely comfortable sitting up on the kitchen table eating his entrée. I ask her if it's a logical progression for a zookeeper to end up with a house full of animals and she softens and smiles.

"Absolutely. It's wonderful. I've got a zoo without cages."

She also runs the lodge as a bed and breakfast, but it's pretty clear the animals are her first priority.

"I'm lucky I get mostly professionals staying here, zoologists and biologists studying the Tablelands or the tree kangaroos, you know, or people who enjoy the animals and know they'll always be my priority.

"I've had a lot of film crews come and stay, as well. One time I had a Striped Possum under care and the BBC somehow heard of this and sent a crew to film it for one of David Attenborough's specials.

"So they set up all their camera gear around a tree out there, and put barriers on the trunk so it wouldn't escape, but sure enough the first time they let it go it climbed straight over their barriers and disappeared into the forest.

* Strangely, at the time, and every time during the editing process that I worked on this chapter or the accompanying DVD story, I had an unprecedented urge to eat cashew nuts.

"Well the producer was distraught and the cameraman kept asking me if it'll come back and everyone was worried they'd come all the way over here for nothing.

"And every so often we'd get a bearing on him in a different part of the forest – he was wearing a tracking device – and the producer would just ring his hands and moan, 'What am I supposed to tell the boss? That we let him go and he just ran away? He'll kill me.'

"But I told them he'd come back when he was ready. And he did, eventually, and ran straight down my blouse."

Of course.

SPY CAMERAS

"Were you a good spy?" I ask him.

"No," he laughs. "Just very average, run-of-the-mill."

"What's the most frightening thing you ever had to do?"

"Sit at an airport in a garbage bin with a lid on, it was stinking hot, I nearly melted, they wanted photos of people getting on and off the plane and there were security guards all over the place."

"Did anyone try to put garbage in your bin?"

"No, thank goodness," he says, laughing at my impertinence.

The man I'm interviewing used to be a spy for the Australian Government. He carried a large pistol stuffed down the front of his shorts and served in Korea. He knows things about national security that would make most of us blanch. Yet he's self-conscious about smiling for the camera because he's knocked out some teeth helping a mate move furniture. It's an intriguing mix. But he's an intriguing man.

He lives in an off-Broadway town in conservative North Queensland and drives a conspicuous red Ferrari. Against all advice he set up a Spy and Camera Museum in the main street. They all said he was crazy. It'd never work.

"Nine years later it's still working," he tells me with a forgivable trace of smug. "People come in – especially from overseas – and can't understand why it's not in a capital city.

"Couples come to the door and the women stay outside thinking it won't interest them, letting the men go in alone. Ten minutes later the men go back outside to get their wives, 'You've got to see this place.' Then the women often come back later with friends, sometimes three, four times."

The 'place' is a treasure chest of spy cameras and paraphernalia, actual photographs taken by spies of military and political targets, deadly sleight-of-hand weapons, authentic Russian Spy IDs, disguises for field equipment – cameras that look like tools, handbags, cigarette lighters, etc – along with a number of very rare collectors cameras dating back to the 1800s. He tells me he's got three thousand cameras in storage, but only exhibits the most significant or unique.

He shows me a buttonhole camera used by the KGB. The lens

is secreted in the top button of an overcoat and wired to a control mechanism in the coat's pocket. When activated you can see the tiny shutters in the centre of the button open and close. It's quaint and a touch theatrical, almost too much like the movies to be real.

He's a man of sixty or more with thinning, snowy hair. He's dressed 'public servant casual' in a short-sleeved blue chambray shirt above belted slacks and shoes. His nose is bent and his complexion is ruddy. Nothing in his appearance gives away his past. But then, that was his past.

He tells me the unusual career began when he was in the artillery corps and got singled out for special duties because he was a fast runner. I got the impression his unit basically had a foot race and the place-getters got to be spies. And presumably the sloggers at the back of the pack became cannon fodder. It's not a race I'd like to run.

"I'd also worked for the Post Office and I knew about communications," he adds. "So I worked in signals in Korea through the war."

"So one minute you were an enlisted soldier and the next you were a spy?"

"Yeah, pretty much. There were sixty of us in the unit."

"Sixty spies? Doing what?" I was having trouble shaking an image of many dark-suited men in sunglasses hiding behind trees.

"Well, we had to cover a shift on the telephone exchange, eight hours on eight hours off. While we were gathering intelligence it had to look like we had normal jobs.

"And the interesting thing was I ended up supplying information to the Americans as well, and none of my colleagues knew."

"Did you know what all of your colleagues were up to?"

He thinks about this for a moment as if considering the possibility he wasn't the only double agent for the very first time, then says, "No, because we answered to an intermediary."

Again I'm surprised how much the game is apparently played according to the movie script, and I ask an almost superfluous and long-winded question about whether the government ever issues commands the public would be horrified to know about.

"Absolutely. All the time."

"I mean we read about this stuff in espionage novels, see it in the movies," I push the point, "how much is real and how much is fiction?"

"I'd say the public know about one percent of what's going on."

"So who does know what's going on?"

"That'd be the Yanks. They've got the satellites in the sky. They can read the newspaper over your shoulder if they want."

"So with the technology available today, do you think spies have got it easy?"

"That's a tough question," he pauses. "I don't think spies have ever got it easy. Not if they get caught." Then he laughs and puts his hand to his mouth to cover the gaps in his teeth.

"What happens then?"

"You've got some drama."

"Did that worry you when you were out there?"

"No, I was young, and fit, and didn't care."

He shows me a photo of the younger, fitter spy with chest bared and gun leveled at an unseen target.

"That was taken in Korea."

"What were you carrying?"

"A forty-five. And it was carried here," he says, patting the flat front of his trousers to the right of his fly. "In the holster inside the pants. And even though it was a big weapon you could hardly see it."

"So you were packing."

"Yeah. Commonly known as hired killers for the Australian Government."

We're conducting this conversation as he gives me a guided tour of the museum. It's a fascinating exhibition in its own right but I'm finding what he has to say even more compelling. He has a way of dropping the occasional unguarded remark into the mix that keeps me on my toes. He shows me the tiny camera he carried in the field, the same one he'd have had with him in the garbage bin at the airport.

"It's a Steky. Japanese-made, a lovely little camera with a long lens." He handles the camera fondly. "So you could put some distance between you and the target."

"Was the camera more important than the gun, or vice versa?"

"The camera was more important because it was hard evidence. A gun'll get rid of evidence; you can shoot it."

"Did you ever…?"

"No," he answers before I've finished asking the question.

"You wouldn't tell me anyway, would you," I say. And through another self-conscious laugh he gives me absolutely no indication of whether he's lying or not.

"We have this impression of spies," I say, "drinking martinis and getting all the girls."

This time he laughs without restraint. "Yeah? That's only once you get out of the organization, mate. And get yourself a fast car and open the door."

And out on the street the fire engine red Ferrari with number plates CIA 007 awaits its owner, an ordinary ex-spy living a low-key civilian life in Smalltown, Queensland.

STILL NOT A COWBOY

Benino's back*. Benino's my daughter who joins me during the school holidays sometimes. It's not automatic anymore – she's twelve years old and has social obligations to manage these days as well as family – so I have to make sure I'm "somewhere really cool, Dad." But she loves the Great Barrier Reef so it's not hard to entice her to Cairns.

* Not her real name – I choose to live in the public eye, she can make her own choices.

Before she gets her promised snorkelling trip to the reef she joins me while I shoot an Atherton Tablelands travelogue. It turns into a big week.

On the way up the ranges we call in at the Cairns Wildlife Safari Reserve with all the usual African suspects in attendance, and Benino gets to hand feed a Cheetah and a couple of Lemurs. Then we visit Granite Gorge and get to feed the largest, laziest colony of Rock Wallabies in the world. Okay, so I'm exaggerating but I doubt by much. Then out of the blue we are invited to stay on a property with a lake full of platypuses, and we get fed pancakes (Benino's favourite) for breakfast the next morning. Our new friend the spy takes her for her first ever spin in a Ferrari. And of course she loves the close contact with the Tree Kangaroos and the possums and especially the Paddy Melons at Lumholtz Lodge.

Like I said, for a young city girl it's been a big week.

But as cool as all this stuff is, what she really wants to do while we're up on the Tablelands is go horse riding. And though she'd never admit it she wants me to go with her.

Now I had a bit to do with horses when I was younger and none of it was pleasant. I ended up bitten, bucked or bounced off almost every horse I encountered and after a while I just gave up trying. I figured the world didn't need another horse lover and it was unlikely the horse world would ever miss me.

For my daughter, though, I would come out of retirement.

"Really?" she said.

"Sure."

"Coooool."

I wasn't so sure.

"Do you want one hour, or two?" the horse lady asks us when we arrive at the stables. Benino looks at me hopefully but I avoid eye contact.

"I think an hour should be plenty."

"The parents often come on the ride once," the lady says knowingly, "then after that they sit and wait at the stables till we get back."

"Sounds good to me," I say, but we both know I'm too far gone now. Benino is already trying on helmets and hanging off every word the horse lady says and I can see she's really into it. I steel myself for the ride.

She gives me an old grey mare called Zoe and I climb aboard. Zoe turns her head and snorts. I quietly assure her the feelings are mutual and we set off.

There are four of us on the ride: the horse lady and her right hand man, and Benino and myself. It's mid-morning and a pleasant time to be walking through the bush on horseback. We flush Button Quail from the side of the track and Black Cockatoos let us approach quite close before flying. The gentle sway of the horse is comforting and I find myself almost enjoying the experience.

Then someone decides it's time to pick up the pace and my reverie is broken. This is the bit I don't like. This is when my natural disinclination for horse riding comes to the fore. This is when it starts to hurt. And to make matters worse this is also when the horse figures out I don't know what I'm doing and starts trying to compensate.

So here's what happens.

First we break into a trot and I bounce along like a ball bearing on tiles, trying to find that elusive up-down, two-for-one rhythm the horse lady has been teaching Benino, and crushing to death every living tadpole in my epididymis.

Soon it's clear a canter is going to be my only salvation, but it's impossible to give a horse a confident command when you're barely hanging on and she's not responding. Indeed she wants to slow down because she knows she's got an arrhythmic clot in the saddle, so she's trying to settle into a murderous jogtrot that smashes my gonads with every step. And I'm now officially in pain.

But somehow I get her into a canter and we're flying along a bush track with branches on either side threatening to knock me off as if I needed any assistance the way I'm lurching from side to side and not necessarily in that order and any second could be my last in contact with Zoe but anything's better than the jogtrot then up ahead I see the right hand man slowing down and Zoe's pulling up as well oh no here we go again-ain-ain-ain-ain-ouch. God I hate horse riding.

Of course I know all this is due to a bad riding technique, but unfortunately that's what I've got and it doesn't really help me to know this. What I'd rather know is who was it decided it was natural for man to sit astride an animal running at speed. It's all wrong: they've got four legs on the ground like they always do and we've got two legs flapping around in the air, two arms trying to look useful and one bum trying to suck it up and hang on. Every bit about it is unnatural, and all I can think of as we finally make it back to the stables is how much I'm looking forward to renewing my vows of retirement.

Then Benino asks me if I had fun and her faced is so flushed with joy I haven't the heart to disappoint her.

"Well, Sweetheart, I survived. And I enjoyed watching you having fun."

"Did Zoe go fast for you? Did she canter?"

"Oh yes, she showed me all her party tricks. How about yours?"

And she tells me excitedly how her horse jumped a log and broke into a canter and almost galloped at one stage, and even though I smile encouragement it all sounds ghastly to me.

"Do you think we can do it again someday?" she asks the dreaded question.

"Well I guess I wasn't planning on having any more children."

"Tomorrow?"

"Tomorrow?" My vas deferens turn inside out. "But what about the reef?"

"Oh, yeah. I forgot."

And I thank the creator anew for the Great Barrier Reef.

UNSPRUNG

It's almost midnight at Innot Hot Springs and the sky is starry and clear. There's a real chill on the air. Inside the bus Benino sleeps the sleep of the mostly innocent, though I'm secretly pleased to say she complained of soreness after our ride today. And I'm sitting outside on my deluxe foldaway ten-dollar camping chair, with only the flying foxes and the bastard Claude for company.

I've taken to calling him the bastard because he continues to be one. He seems to be working his way through every auto-electrical problem known to motor vehicles at present. There's a gremlin in the system, no question, but nobody seems to be able to find it. I even lost my temper in front of my daughter tonight and that's not something I'm proud of. There are enough bad examples around without her father setting more.

Right now, though, I'm contemplating a walk down to the creek to test the recuperative powers of the hot springs. It's said they'll cure anything from arthritis to liver failure. I'm hoping they'll work on auto-electrical psychosis as well.

There's an information board out the front that claims back in the 1890s Innot was a very happening place. Apparently there were two hotels and a bathhouse operating here, and a weekly service from Atherton. You can almost imagine the dandies from Atherton boarding the coach for their yearly purge, all top hats and tails, petticoats and bustles. I guess it was the nineteenth century's equivalent of a health retreat.

During that period the spring water was so feted it was barrelled and transported over the ranges to Townsville for bottling. Some was even exported to Europe for medicinal purposes. That's what the sign says, anyway. But the sign also has a picture of a voluptuous young woman reclining on her side in the springs and I never saw her anywhere this afternoon, so maybe it's just more spin to keep the tourists entertained.

It's unlikely the present owners would be overly concerned, either way. When I arrived I told them I was going to include Innot Hot Springs in the Tourism Australia package and the woman said, "Doesn't help us any. We're leaving. That'll be twenty-seven dollars for the site, thanks."

Freebies aren't essential with this gig but they do tend to go hand-in-hand with gratis publicity, in this case even if only as a gesture of goodwill for the incoming owners. But maybe I'm being unkind and they've simply had enough, done their best but reached the end of their tether. I imagine when it's time to leave a place like this you can't get out quickly enough. It could use a breath of fresh air, anyway, some new energy.

Meantime I'm not sure I've got the energy to get myself down to the creek for a dip in the all-healing springs. It's not far, but I'm finding it hard to imagine taking my clothes off in the cool night air. I'd maybe do it for the woman on the billboard, or what I could see of her, at least, which is not much more than her back. But like I said, she didn't make herself known to me when I arrived so it's unlikely she'll be down there now.

The other deterrent is the blackness of the night. It might be starry and wonderful up there in the sky, but down here it's as black as a dead fly and I'd be likely to walk right into the creek. In some pools it's supposed to be hot enough to boil eggs, and I don't like the thought of that after what I did to them today.

We head back to Cairns tomorrow so I can take Benino for her reef dive. Then I put her on a plane for home. As usual the time has passed too quickly. And as usual I start questioning what I'm doing out here missing out on so much of her life.

I cooked fish and chips for dinner tonight, the best she's ever had, she said. The fish was Spangled Emperor from Sweers Island and the chips turned out brown and crisp. We ate them sitting in our deck chairs as night fell. Benino even ate three micrograms of salad. It's the little things you miss the most.

And it's not just missing my daughter that makes me question this path I've chosen; it's the validity of it as well. Sometimes I think I must be as mad as people say I am. Does anyone really care that these stories are told, that the country is charted through its people? And am I good enough to do the whole thing justice anyway? I don't know.

Artists take consolation in the fact that self-doubt goes with the territory and all artists think their work isn't good enough at some stage of their careers. But what if they're right? And surely most must be right, most of the time, going by the scarce few works that survive, mustn't they? Again, I don't know.

I do know it's time for bed, though. All this introspection is not good for the focus.

WHAT BUS?

So Benino gets her trip to the reef and spends every available second in the water and comes home looking like a cooked prawn in spite of my efforts to keep sunscreen on her translucency and I know her mother will go crook at me never mind we've been divorced over a decade now mothers still retain the right to administer justice to ex-husbands if they see fit and it seems their eyesight improves with distance.

Luckily Benino knows of a miracle salve she can apply to ease the burn and take away the redness but it's already five o'clock when the boat docks and the chemists will all be shut except maybe the one at Cairns Central so I pull a radical angle park in a narrow space next to the bus bay and Benino runs across the road to buy her medicine be quick sweetheart be quick I'm illegally parked here and off she goes and I'm tired and cranky from a day at sea being told where I could and couldn't dive by a bunch of kids who weren't even born when I first dived on the reef and the bus drivers are giving me the evil eye and honking as they angle in to pick up their passengers at the stop when some woman taps on my windscreen and says I've hit her car with my bus of all things I didn't need.

What bus is all I can think of to say what bus even though it's blatantly obvious she's not talking about the 351 to Innisfail but she ignores my nonsense and keeps on at me like I've ruined her life until I've got no choice but to deny it point blank which puts her on the back foot momentarily before some nosy parker with shopping bags comes up and confirms I did hit the thing she saw it move as I parked Jesus wept wouldn't that floor you a reliable witness right now just when I'm about to take oath and swear I never touched a lick of her car the mark is so small anyway haven't you got anything better to do than pick on poor harassed fathers of sunburned children on the streets of Cairns for Christ's sake?

Now normally I'd handle such an event with a whole lot more grace after all the lady *was* in the right and a smiling apology goes a long way under those circumstances anyway it's not as if I can pretend to be anyone else with my face plastered all over Claude's unsubtle exterior but once she starts accusing me of lying to her by denying I've hit her car I have no option but to keep on lying and pretty soon I'm telling her I'm so sure I didn't hit her car I reckon I might have even been parked there before she arrived and maybe *she* hit *me* what do you think of that for a scenario little Miss End-of-the-World how about that for a curved ball?

But she's either too smart or too stubborn to buy into my game and just looks at me like I'm some kind of moron then starts up her carping again I'm really beginning to dislike this woman almost enough to give her my whole it's only a bloody motor car so what if it gets scratched the world would be a better place without them anyway spiel but I decide I'd be wasting my breath shoppers don't see any connection between consumption and global warming so instead I pull my license from my wallet with a defiant flourish and say there do what you like I don't care you might as well get the system to harvest just a little more grist from my bones before I die.

Then help comes from an unexpected quarter in the form of Nosy Parker who senses I'm like a cornered animal on the verge of snapping whether I'm a moron or not and she starts soothing

Miss End-of-the-World it's only a scorch mark it'll buff out it'll be fine look how it comes off when I rub it and I'm impressed she knows so much about car restoration and wonder for an inappropriate moment how she is with auto-electrics but before I get a chance to propose marriage I sense Miss End-of-the-World backing off so I retract my license jump back in the driver's seat close the door behind me and try to find somewhere else to look but into Miss End-of-the-World's face now peering at me through the front windscreen.

Now all this has taken long enough for Benino to sample the entire range of anti-sunburn cosmetics from every country in the world yet still she hasn't returned and Miss End-of-the-World is banging on about being in a hurry to get out when she can see clearly there are three buses lined up on the street waiting to pull in and neither of us could get out even on a skateboard for fuck's sake whatever happened to good old fashioned patience I want to know and I want to know right now.

But soon Benino's back and the buses are clearing and I can finally get out of this Godforsaken mess so I'm trying to reverse out on the same trajectory I entered to show once and for all it wasn't me your honour drove into that silly woman's car but of course I nearly hit her car again so I have to do a seven-point juggle to get out which makes it obvious I hit the bloody thing and little Miss End-of-the-World is watching with a measured I-told-you-so grin on her face and life's just not fair when you're wrong and everyone else is right like I said to the young kid on the Telstra no-help desk the other day it's no wonder people get frustrated and shoot other people these days but he just went really quiet on the other end of the line.

And Benino shows me the magic gel and says it was cheap only ten dollars and I say don't worry I paid out here on the street and she asks me what I mean but I say your father just had a brain snap don't worry about it so she doesn't I know because she immediately spots a Beetle but I tell her I don't want to play right now I must be in a real funk because I love playing Beetles with her but I'm too busy concentrating on avoiding other cars and giving myself a hard time for being such a jerk and wondering about a world where material possessions are everything and everyone is wound up so tight we can't even deal with a simple skirmish on the streets without acrimony and why I can't seem to spend more than a day or two in the real world before I'm at odds with the thing I've got to get out of this place and go somewhere with enough space for a man and his seven metre bus called Claude.

DOUBLE FIGURES

And speaking of buses, I was sitting in a café recently when a man approached me and asked if that was my bus parked out front. I said yes his name is Claude would you like to take him home.

He said no thanks he was right for buses since he already had one twice as big.

But he didn't seem like the kind of bloke to indulge in one-upmanship so I pursued the matter and asked how big his family was.

"Eleven," he said like it was nothing much, like they were really just beginning and could end up twenty if the weather stayed fine.

I couldn't think of anything to say for several seconds. Eleven sounded like a very big number to me. Mentally I was trying to fit them all inside Claude but they kept poking out the holes. When I finally did speak I displayed all my genius.

"So you've got nine kids?"

I could tell he was impressed just by the slow way he nodded. Then he showed me a photo from his wallet of the family lined up against bus and I noticed it was a very big bus indeed just to accommodate them all standing up along the *outside*, never mind all the sleeping and eating and washing and the many other human activities associated with living *inside* a bus. And he went on to tell me how they were from the west and they'd been bussing around the country for a couple of years but they were now looking to move to the Atherton Tablelands to settle for a while.

Two years, nine kids, one bus, I had to do a story on this family. I asked if he'd be interested and he said he'd consult with his wife and get back to me. For their sake I hoped that didn't lead to any more children.

Several days later I pulled up alongside their bus with the whole family gathered to meet me. It was a lovely, warm greeting and it made me feel like Queen Elizabeth, or at very least Snow White. There were kids everywhere, ranging from teenagers to toddlers, all well presented and polite. And standing in the middle wearing beatific grins was a couple in their mid-thirties looking way too young to be responsible for such a contribution.

"And there's another one on the way," was the first thing the woman said to me. I would've uttered a blasphemous expletive only it was clear from the slogans painted on the side of their bus that these people were Christians. Instead I let the genius out for another run.

"Ten?" I said.

"Maybe more," she smiled. "We'll see."

Well that was it for me; I'd run out of fingers. I had to change the subject before I was caught out, so I suggested a cook's tour.

Their rig was an old Denning 11 metre, 280hp 2-stroke Detroit diesel ex-school bus, behind which they towed a troop carrier and dinghy on a trailer. Two slide-out panels gave them extra width in the dining area and kids bedroom when stationary, and ranked as one of the three features they couldn't do without. I think the other two were the instantaneous gas hot water system and the coffee machine.

The front of the bus was standard, with steps leading up to the driver's seat and a 'dicky seat' to the right of the steps. Immediately behind the open cabin came the lounge and dining table where the kids sat and did schoolwork while they travelled – "except when the scenery is interesting" – which faced a galley-style kitchen equipped with full oven, five-burner cook top and range hood, and plenty of under-bench cupboard space. Opposing fridge and pantry with a connecting door between gave the option to cordon off the area from the bedrooms and completed that section.

Next came the kids' bedroom with three levels of bunk beds, a foldaway table bed and a portable cot. And as cliché as it may be, listening to Mum outline the sleeping arrangements it was hard to shake the image of packing sardines.

"Two children go here, toe to toe, then two children go on the next one, toe to toe, and then one bit bigger one goes down the bottom one. And then we have a safe cot here, and that gets set up for the baby each night. And then we have this bed here…" etc.

Across the passage was the bathroom, with bath, shower *and* flush toilet.

"That's important," Mum tells me. "I would not want to empty a port-a-loo every day."

"*You* wouldn't want to? *I* wouldn't want to!" Dad chimes in, leaving no doubt about who'd get that job if it were up for grabs.

Mum laughs and moves us on to the last section.

"And this is our sanctuary; it's got a door," she says, prioritising. "And a queen-sized bed."

"And you've always got a different view out the window," says Dad.

Their bedroom has a small wardrobe in one corner and a dresser of sorts opposite, an air conditioner and one small shelf. I didn't notice any overhead cupboards.

"You don't need as much clothes and shoes as you think you do. I have all my clothes in one little draw. And so does Troy. And everyone was allowed to bring two pairs of shoes."

"Which brings me to my next question. When you do settle down, are you going to spread out?"

They both answered at once in the overwhelming affirmative.

"Oh yeah."

"Absolutely."

"We're just about at the end of our bus travelling days."

"Two-and-a-half years is a good stint for anyone with lots of kids."

"Our youngest was born here in the Tablelands, in the bus."

"We had a busbirth, with a midwife."

"But number ten will be at home."

I make a mental note not to go there again and ask instead about the highs and lows.

"Well, the high points are you're enriching their lives for the rest of their lives. Before we left, Troy and I had never been out of the state, and now our kids have been to every state in the country."

"But I think the normal trials of life are intensified all the time, living in a bus."

"You're trying to make dinner and someone's in the way, and someone's got their laptop out, and someone else is trying to do their homework…"

"And you can't walk around asking people to hop out of your way all the time…"

"With every child you have you let go of a little of the 'Oh, I used to be able to have long baths, and I used to go for walks' and you give in to becoming a mum and a dad and having demands, you know?"

"Do you think it's made you better people?"

Again came the dual affirmation.

"Yeah, I reckon."

"It's good character building."

"And because we're Christians we have to ask for God's help every day."

"Not be be grumpy, and to be more patient . . ."

"Like everyone, we struggle with all sorts of things, you know."

And I don't know too much about their man at the top but I'd hazard a guess he'd cut them some slack. I seem to remember he had a soft spot for things by the dozen.

THE ROAD ALWAYS WINS

In the end it was the wind blew me out of Cairns. After a week of next-to-zero knots – perfect conditions for taking daughters to the reef and getting them lobstered – it picked up its skirts and started to dance. At every glimpse of the sea all the way to Cooktown one of the most beautiful coastal stretches we have was grey and chopped, and the rainforest – normally lush and sensuous – was about as dry as it gets. It wasn't an unpleasant drive, but if I were seeing it for the first time I might have been wondering what all the fuss was about.

In Cooktown it rained: big, fat drops that raised the dust and promised more than they could ever deliver. I counted them and still had fingers left to cross. I didn't want it to rain, not at this stage of the trip. None of the usual signs pointed to an early wet season, but if I learned one thing doing weather for fifteen years it was that weather doesn't read the signs. I headed north with one eye on the road and one on the sky*.

I was advised to avoid the coast road to Cape Melville and to take the Battle Camp Road instead. That suited me because I wanted to see if there was anyone at the Vietnam Veterans Camp on Kalpowar Station who would talk to me. The camp had been set up on a disused section of the cattle station by ex-Bush Tucker Man Major Les Hiddons to give the Vets somewhere to get away from the rat race, and there'd been an ongoing dispute over its right to exist there before everything went quiet a couple of years ago. Whether it had gone quiet because the battle had been lost or won I never learned, because I never made it to Kalpowar.

Corrugations are expected on these roads, even in long stretches. There's usually a float speed you can reach and basically plane above the ruts, although it can be perilous making sure the dips don't catch you going too fast. When that happens you'll likely hit your head on something in the cabin – the ceiling, the windscreen, your passenger's head – depending on how your suspension behaves. Some vehicles bottom out in holes, Claude lurches like a drunk then bounces along like an overweight balloon for a hundred metres. But however it responds, rest assured corrugations will test every fixing on your vehicle and anything the least bit suspect will get shaken off. As someone said to me at the time, the road always wins.

* Lucky I didn't crash, really, driving cross-eyed like that.

Naturally I had my share of problems along the way, but none so freakish as one I authored myself. Leaving Cooktown I turned the inverter on and put my main camera battery on charge. When I do this I sit the battery/charger unit on a tea towel in the sink to cushion it somewhat and avoid creating a missile in the back. But somehow, incredibly, the unit bounced up and turned on the tap, the tea towel blocked the plughole, the sink filled with water and the bloody thing drowned itself! Amazing what technology can do these days.

I knew nothing of this, of course, until I pulled over after a particularly savage section to do an inspection and discovered not only the front bumper and one blinker unit falling off, but also water dripping from under the back door where it had no right being in the first place. And to add insult to injury the bus wouldn't re-start.

To cut a long and dusty story short if it wasn't for the help of an ex-truckie from Cairns I'd still be looking for the broken lead from the battery to the starter motor – which had frayed apart, thanks again to the corrugations – and to resolve the other problem I had to backtrack to Mareeba to buy a new charger. Remarkably, the lithium battery survived the live submersion and continued to work perfectly once dried out.

This time when I headed north I went straight up the Peninsula Development Road and it was like driving on a highway by comparison. Either I got lucky with my timing or they've spent a lot of money upgrading, but it was nothing like the road I took to the tip in the early nineties. I guess it's only a matter of time before the main road is sealed all the way to the tip and the Cape as a last frontier will be changed forever, which in many ways will be a shame. For it's been the tyranny of distance created by the road conditions that has protected many of the Cape's endangered species. And I don't just mean the flora and fauna, but the people who've been left alone to "expand to fill the available space", the human colour of the place.

Like Charlie the Maltese miner in Coen, for instance, who reputedly uses chooks to mine gold.

Charlie came to Coen twenty-five years ago to take a three-month break from his family. His leasehold was originally a company concern that he took over when the gold dried up. Though he no longer operates the mine Charlie still sluices a bit of alluvial gold for the tourists who come to stay at his quirky bottle house campground.

A good head of hair and a healthy tan make him look young for his sixty-odd years, but the missing teeth give him away in the act of smiling; something he does often.

Another thing he does often is spin a bit of bullshit for the tourists. Problem is he forgets what he said to whom and usually doesn't bother qualifying his audience first.

"I had these people here once," he says, speaking with a rich Old World accent, "and I told them the way I mine gold here is to let the chooks do all the work. They scratch around and pick up the shiny specks, the bigger nuggets get caught in their craw, and when they start walking a bit sideways I knock them on the head and get an ounce of gold.

"Well it turns out they were from ABC radio, and next thing I've got people ringing up wanting to bring five hundred chooks with them to do a bit of mining!

"And they told the story better than I told them: they had me sitting on an esky drinking stubbies and sticking the empties in the wall, building the house out of bottles as I watch for the chooks to start leaning over."

The house is, indeed, a work of art, built over the original mine shaft out of rock quarried from the property, with feature walls of bottles and stained glass windows in keystone arches scalloping the pale blue rendered exterior. The campground, too, is dotted with original statues and oddities (can't think of a better word) Charlie has entertained himself making out of bits and pieces of crap (ditto) during the quiet wet season months. The whole setup is a quirky manifestation of Charlie's personality with cheeky signs highlighting his irreverence – the toilets are signposted "4 U 2 P" and provide options for "His shaft" and "Her tunnel" – and for my money it offers a welcome change from the usual bland, mainstream offering. But the star of this exhibition is definitely the man himself.

"I had a German film crew come through here a couple of years ago doing a documentary on the Cape, and they found that cross I've got in the ground over there and asked me what it was for. And I told them it was for the last bitch I had here she fell down the shaft and collapsed it when she hit the bottom.

"'Is she still down there?' they ask me, so I tell them 'Of course. And I didn't push her either. She go too close to edge and fall herself.' And on like that, you know.

"Anyway, soon I start getting letters and phone calls from overseas, from women wanting to come out and work my jackhammer for me and other wild proposals. Apparently I also said to the camera that I need a replacement to help me keep my shaft clean or some bullshit like that."

And there are many other amusing stories he enjoys re-telling given the opportunity, no doubt embellishing them with each delivery, but all is not jolly in Charlie's world.

Like all miners he has a "near miss" story, involving a disputed claim over a rich seam of gold, a mysterious illness and a blown mine shaft to settle the dispute once and for all time, and while I have no way of knowing how much was fact and how much was paranoid fiction neither did he give me any reason to doubt him. And while he claims a more innocent motivation, at least one of his approach signs seems to be tainted with the bitterness of an old feud*.

In addition his lease is up for renewal next year and he's been given no indication it will be extended. Indeed the McIlraith handover** in 2008 has made him suspicious that the official line is now for all securable land on the Cape to be handed back to the traditional owners as leases expire.

And to complicate matters the tourism authorities are pressuring him to get accreditation to operate as a *bona fide* tourist destination and, logically, he refuses to spend any money on the necessary upgrades unless his lease is secured, so he's in quandary.

"At this moment I'm bit lost, actually," he tells me. "I'm still

* Second colour section, page 7, bottom.

** 180,000 hectares of land around Coen was handed back to the traditional owners to be jointly operated with Queensland National Parks & Wildlife as an Aboriginal-owned National Park.

doing what I'm doing, but if they don't give me secure for the land I just bulldoze everything and go back to Malta. At least I have a country to go to.

"I'm forty years in this country but I'm sorry I become Australian, because we're not looked after anymore."

I ask him if he thinks we're becoming too bureaucratized and open up the floodgates, with Charlie railing about everything from liability insurance to road conditions, government indifference to the proliferation of red tape, with the neglect of the tourism industry on the Cape coming in for the most serious serve.

"But when the tourists come here they love it," he says, his smile returning, "I tell them a bit of bullshit about chooks and they love that, you know. They forget about the politics then."

But I suspect what he's really saying is *he* forgets about the politics then.

Either way the road still wins.

PARADISE OFFERED

"Most of them have no idea how difficult it can be here." He opens up a profile on his computer. "Here's a woman with children in Sydney and Melbourne, has close family ties, and she's new to Australia so she's going to be wanting to see her kids all the time. And you can't just whiz down and see the kids every weekend from here."

"Do any of them get lascivious with their responses?"

"Oh yeah, one woman wanted tantric sex. And there's a bird here – I must have hit the X button or something – and she wants to do massages and eroticky-type stuff."

I'd heard about this man long before I met him: a high flyer from Sydney who'd dropped out to come and live on a tropical island in far north Queensland. There'd also been some media attention about his quest to find a mate. "Robinson Crusoe seeks girl Friday" was the gist of the coverage. But I wanted to meet the man and decide for myself what was cliché and what was real.

We arrange for him to collect me from the beach opposite his island and I watch as he crosses the narrow passage in his dinghy – plenty of white hair, brown skin, blue water, yellow sand; all very real so far.

He moves efficiently but without grace as he clambers to the bow and tosses the anchor overboard, then returns to the outboard motor to reverse in; like a man who's done it many times before but wasn't born to it in the first place. He reaches out to take my camera as I jump in and lift the anchor. The dinghy is half way across the channel before we say "G'day".

To greet us at the island is his dangerously excitable pup, Quasi, a Ridgeback-something cross that almost capsizes the dinghy trying to climb in before we hit the beach. He's pleased to see us.

At first glance the island presents an assortment of ramshackle buildings on a small flat area at the base of a rocky hill. Coconut palms line the beach and casuarinas and assorted frangipanis grow between the white sand and the native vegetation at the foot of the slope. Whole dried coconuts are stacked in piles here and there, and barnacled buoys and ropes and fragments of netting hang from the weatherworn frame of the nearest structure. An old wooden boat lays tilted to one side just above high water mark. It seems a perfect island hideaway setting.

Over a cup of tea my host tells me he first came to the island with a girlfriend about fifteen years ago but she wasn't able to handle the pace and left.

"I got whacked in the stock market crash of '87, my marriage fell apart, and I'd found a new woman and was looking for something different to do."

"So you rang up a real estate agent and said, 'Find me an island.'"

"Effectively, yeah. But it's hard here. Water's an issue obviously, there's no soil – it's basically volcanic boulders and sand. And you can't jump in the car and drive to the shops whenever you feel like it. I don't blame her for leaving."

Since then he's been living on his own, apart from Quasi the dog, and the occasional travelling WWOOFer coming to help him out for a few weeks or a month before moving on.

He gives me the cook's tour of the island and identifies the various outbuildings – there's a bungalow called The Love Shack, an open-sided room with a view of the water from the double bed; the Beach Bar I'd seen when we first landed, where he has BBQs for guests and serves home brewed beer; a shed he's establishing an art workshop in for the local indigenous mob; a strange-looking fibreglass donga he's converted into more accommodation quarters; a beachfront bungalow he's planning to turn into a restaurant – and he shows me his garden with some pride.

"We have to mulch everything down to make soil," he says, taking a handful of the coarse dirt and letting it run through his fingers, "so I get the prawn trawlers to save me their waste, as well as what I make. Takes about twelve months to break down, but in the wet season we can grow all the Asian vegetables, bananas, yams, and I keep a small herb garden going through the dry."

Like all gardeners he finds little things to do as we walk – a palm frond is tossed on the compost heap, a frangipani flower is plucked from its branch and sniffed as we pass, a misplaced rock is repositioned in a retaining wall, a shovelful of soil is turned over in its bed – and I can't help noticing one of the gardens is heart-shaped.

"Yeah," he laughs, but gives no explanation.

Back at his home he shows me the insulated bath he's built, and the outdoor shower and the colourful laundry and toilet, all of which have been decorated with a woman's eye.

"I've had a young WWOOFer here helping me with the feminine touches. First thing she did when she arrived was attacked the bathroom and toilet. 'How can you expect a woman to put up with such primitive facilities?' She told me. So I built the bath, and she's painted everything, added the decorations. 'If you want to attract a woman you have to make it nice,' she says."

It's clear he's nesting, and that's when I raise the subject again. "There seems to be a recurring theme going on here. You've got Love Shacks, heart-shaped yam gardens… do you think there's something missing?"

He laughs generously. "Well there is. I haven't even shown you Miranda yet, but I've got a manikin here."

I admitted I'd already seen Miranda, a scrawny-arsed shop dummy with a pasty complexion and bad dress sense, and would've mentioned it earlier only the handcuffs she was wearing put me off.

"Yeah, she gets moved around a bit, between being tied to trees, and boats, and bedrooms, and kitchen tables… only problem is she's inanimate."

"So you miss female company?"

"Of course you do, it's natural, it's normal, it's good."

"You don't think that'd ruin it for you? Having a woman around?"

"Man seeks love of a woman, and that's what drives him. Everything he holds dear is female – nature, mother earth – the things precious to us we give female names."

He's got it bad. And it's no surprise he decided to go online to try and find love through the Internet.

"I've had a lot of enquiries, and interest," he says, showing me a sampling of letters and photos women have sent him. "And you realise there's a lot of crazy people out there. But there are also a lot of people desperate for change."

But so far he's had no joy. And the man's serious about finding a partner. I know quite a number of married men who'd envy his lifestyle, living barefoot and shirtless on a tropical island, growing your own vegetables and bartering home brewed beer for fresh prawns and crayfish from the trawlers, no deadlines to meet and nobody to answer to but yourself. But after fifteen years of it this man's ready for a woman in his life and he doesn't mind what he has to do to find her.

"I'll go anywhere," he tells me, "supermarkets, libraries, museums, operas…"

"Supermarkets are very good," I say, as if I've suddenly become the guru on all matters female. "All women shop."

"Well I could go to shoe shops, and bra shops, that's where women go too."

"No. Blokes hanging around bra shops doesn't work. You'll look like a pervert."

"Doesn't work? Look, I have a very simple brief. I'm looking for an intelligent, feminine, adventurous woman with an open mind. Most women want a real man, well I reckon I'm a real man, so…"

"So bring it on."

"So I want a real woman! But I'm not fixed about how or where or why and I don't mind if she doesn't speak the language, we can sort that stuff out…"

And his pitch goes on well into the night and even the next morning as he ferries me back across to the mainland, and I hope for his sake he finds someone soon. It'd be a shame to see all that peace go to waste.

WHEN BIRDS PLAY

One of the most poetic sights I've ever seen in nature was a flock of Shining Starlings flying offshore to roost on a nearby island. The birds numbered in their many hundreds, perhaps even thousands, and created such wondrous shapes in the afternoon sky as you might see generated by a computer programmed to explore ellipses and parabolas and the possibility of the never-ending plane. Just as they whirled and dipped to form one perfect, nameless shape, the flock would change direction and metamorphose into another equally astounding formation, as the birds revelled in the sheer pleasure of flying. And there could be no other reason for it: the distance between the mainland and the island was no more than a few hundred metres, yet the spectacle lasted over twenty minutes. In some ways it reminded me of an aerial fireworks display, yet even the best New Year's Eve show couldn't match the spontaneous beauty of this silent symphony in the sky.

I saw this at Chili Beach in Iron Range National Park on the east coast of the Cape, a sight made all the more special because I had no forewarning of its occurrence. I was camped at Chili and happened across it naturally. Later I noticed the roosting was even mentioned on my Hema road map, so it's obviously been a feature for travellers for many years, and deservedly so.

Another glorious sight on offer at Iron Range is the Magnificent Riflebird displaying on his perch in the rainforest. A spectacular looking bird in the first instance with his black satin sheen and metallic turquoise bib, the mature male performs at selected sites throughout his territory in order to attract females to mate with. It's a ritual worth spending the time to catch. In a virtuoso performance lasting anything up to an hour he bobs and skips and hops along his perch like a shiny black clown, sometimes moving sideways or backwards with his head down and bum up, at others standing tall and ruffling or preening his feathers, projecting towards an audience he knows or at least hopes is watching. Occasionally he will wolf whistle, the calls ringing loud and clear through the forest, but mostly he concentrates on his dance steps as if he knows it's all in the moves, baby, all in the moves. Then when finally he catches another bird's attention he really turns it on: the wings go up to form a rustling arc above his head, the bobbing intensifies and he starts swaggering from side to side, and with every bouncing pirouette his iridescent breast patch flashes like a jewel and you can't take your eyes off him. He's a pretty boy, all right, and it's little wonder they call him a Bird of Paradise.

But like many before me I've come to Iron Range to see the Eclectus Parrot and the Palm Cockatoo, and hopefully a Cus Cus or two. These rainforests have much in common with Papua & New Guinean habitats – harking back to a time when the countries shared a land bridge across the Strait – and nature lovers the world over come to Cape York specifically to see the exotic flora and fauna.

While I'm in the vicinity I hear of a young woman researching the calls of the Palm Cockatoo so I track her down. She's a delightful creature in her own right and if bird watching still carries a daggy image she could single-handedly give it a sexy overhaul. Born and bred in Los Angeles, USA, she put herself through college on basketball scholarships and has the physique of Aphrodite and the olive-skinned beauty of Carmen (only with short hair and a warm personality). Organising to go out with her for a day in the field feels almost duplicitous.

She originally accepted a scholarship to come to Australia to study snakes but switched to Palm Cockatoos when she decided the bird needed more attention. When I ask her if she's happy with the career jump she says she'll jump to wherever she feels she can have a maximum impact on conservation.

"Things are goin' off the map like that, eh," she says, snapping her fingers.

But it's not her motivation that impresses me the most about this woman; it's her passion. When she speaks about the Cockatoo she is engaging, enthusiastic and articulate, almost to the point where the listener gets lost in a trance just watching her lips move. We're crouched together amongst the ashes of a recent fire keeping vigil on a potentially active nesting hollow and the fact that most of our talking is done in a whisper does nothing to reduce the intimate tone of the interview.

"One of the most interesting things about the Palm Cockatoo," she tells me, "is that they're the only non-human species known to create a tool in a non-foraging context.

"Jane Goodall shocked the world by showing us how chimpanzees fashioned tools to get termites, right? And you see New Caledonian Crows making sticks to get to grubs; that's tool making.

"But when the Palm Cockatoo fashions a drum stick to bang on the hollow it has nothing to do with eating. And that's unique among the entire animal kingdom*.

* Australian scientists have recently discovered an octopus that carries a coconut shell to hide in when threatened – another example of 'tool use' in the animal kingdom.

"It's all part of his territorial behaviour. Sometimes you see the males chomp off about fifteen centimetres of a live eucalyptus branch and fly with it to the display hollow and start drumming," she says, miming the action.

"Exactly why they're doing it is speculative, of course, but the drumming has a certain acoustics to it and they turn their heads to listen, 'Oh no that's not a good spot', and they'll move around to another spot and drum again, then listen," again acting out the scene for me as she speaks.

"We think they're probably saying to any prospective mate in the vicinity, 'Hey, listen to this one, it's a live tree, it's not going to fall over in a cyclone, or burn down in a fire.' As you can see it's fire prone country around here." (The scarcity of suitable hollows means any nesting sites lost to fire can have a real impact on the breeding season.)

"Also, the drumming tells other males there's already a male in this territory, this hollow is taken, stay away.

"It's been recorded in the past where other males have come in and usurped a hollow and smashed the fledgling in the nest, because it takes so long to build the nest it's a huge advantage if they can steal one."

While all we see is the entrance to the nest there's plenty of work goes into making a hollow suitable for egg laying. First the cavity, which might extend all the way to the ground, must be filled with sticks of up to a metre in length to raise the base and give it good drainage in the wet, before the nest platform of splintered sticks and twigs is built on top of that. The process can take many months to complete and it's not hard to see why some birds prefer to outsource the work. This may not do much to aid their poor reproductive rate – along with the Eclectus Parrot they are among the parrot world's least efficient breeders – but it probably increases their collective intelligence.

Carmen of LA is specifically studying their repertoire of calls. And while she stops short of making unqualified statements I get the feeling she rates the birds as smart, suggesting the wide variety of calls they use indicates a complex level of communication, quite apart from their ritualistic use of tools to a degree bettered only by humans.

"Further up the Cape at Moreton Telegraph Station," she says, "I have friends who swear they've seen the birds pruning the Beach Almond trees. Why would they do that if not to produce a heavier crop next year?"

But these are matters for academics to debate; all I know is I'm finding them difficult birds to approach and videotape and I spend all morning in the field without success. Much of the country we cover has been burnt out and the light green shirt I chose to wear as camouflage in the rainforest stands out against the blackened fringe country. I feel like a novice beside the muted purple and khaki worn by Carmen and her field assistant.

During the heat of the day we return to Carmen's shack on the edge of the rainforest, where she lives during the dry season months when she's studying the birds. It's a humble, open-sided affair made available to travelling researchers like Carmen. Creature comforts are few, and apart from a small herb garden there's little sign of permanence. She sleeps in a small bedroom annexed off the larger room and works at a desk set up in the middle of the latter. There is no mains power and she charges her laptop with portable solar panels she moves around to catch the best of the sun.

While we wait for the cool of the afternoon she shows me some of her work. There are several good recordings of the birds' calls – which she tags with descriptive names like "hello" and "double whistle" and "pop toy" (?) – although she says she needs more samples to draw any scientific conclusions. She also has a number of excellent still photographs that travelling photojournalists have gifted her and some shaky but very instructive video recordings she's taken on her own digital camera. In addition she's collected several "drum sticks" and seedpods of the *Grevillea glauca* – commonly known as the bushman's clothes peg – that the birds have used in their acoustic displays.

At about three in the afternoon we head back into the field. This time we keep away from the burnt slopes of the morning's foray and I've swapped my green shirt for a putrid khaki number I retrieved from the dirty clothes basket. I may stink, but at least this time I look the part.

We're rewarded almost immediately. As we approach a site she hasn't visited for some time Carmen turns back to me excitedly and gives the thumbs up. Inadvertently we've approached quite close to the nest and through a stand of saplings I can clearly see a bird sitting quietly on the rim of an upright hollow. The red cheek patch is on full display indicating the bird is not at all anxious about us. When they're less than content the birds cover their patch with cheek feathers, so the signs are good we'll get a voyeur's view of whatever happens. And what happens is this:

After about twenty minutes of sitting patiently on the rim, the bird (the female) takes a long look into the hollow then climbs aside to give her mate – who's been incubating all day – room to climb out. He does so and after the most cursory of handovers leaves her to it, obligingly dipping below, then up and over the camera's field of vision as he flies off. Then she climbs head first down the spout and the show's over.

It's not much in this thrill-obsessed world but it's enough to impress the rapt audience. As I've learnt the Palm Cockatoo is an elusive bird and to see the nest exchange from such close quarters is a real treat, not to mention the positive indication of a successful brood on the way.

"Very, very exciting," Carmen says. "And really rare to see that. I've been studying this bird for five months, morning, afternoon, every single day, and I've seen that activity only twice, that's the second time. So, I'm pretty stoked on that.

"To me, they seem like a very experienced pair. They're a very long-lived bird so they've probably done this many times before. And they've got it down pat, eh. Go in, have a look, switch out, gone. Not even a kiss goodbye."

CUT OFF A LIMB

Sometimes you just get lucky. Sometimes, even in the unlikeliest places, a little ship comes in. On this trip it was at Captain Billy Landing on the far northeast coast of Cape York.

The Landing was named after a blackfella who showed the location to one of the early explorers then later attacked him ("If I show you I'll have to kill you" perhaps?) and these days you access it via a narrow bush track winding through some pretty rainforest country. It's about thirty kilometres off the main Cape road and it's not a difficult run in, just a few bumps and grinds and a dry creek crossing or two, though the wet season would doubtless make it a different proposition, and I fancy the grader had been through not long before me so I timed it well. There's a shelter at the campground festooned with buoys and messages from previous visitors and judging by the boasting comments they've made it has been a challenge at certain times. And they all proudly mention what sort of 4x4 they drove as if it's important to fly the flag, and how much worse the road was when they did it *last* time. Though at least one traveler shared the utter desperation of his situation. On the 15th of May 2009 Pommie wrote simply, "No beer left." I hope you made it, Pommie.

By the time I reached the campground I was worn out. The heavy shooting schedule combined with the late nights spotlighting for Cus Cus and the early mornings editing and writing had done me in. I was in need of somewhere to hole up for a spell to re-charge my batteries and this looked as good as any. And since I had the place all to myself I decided to put the awning out and set up a real camp for the first time this trip. (That's a fair indication of how often I prop for more than one day. It's a great lifestyle working for yourself but the boss can be a hard taskmaster.)

Once set up I went for a bit of an explore, but there's not much there save the remnants of the old landing and some windswept Pacific coastline. I caught a couple of crabs and had a half-hearted fish – too much weed to get serious – then went for a wander up the beach and got annoyed by the amount of human garbage there was along the high tide mark: plastic bottles mainly, a few rubber thongs, children's toys, toothbrushes, even a small refrigerator believe it or not. The highlight was finding a large gas bottle I thought for a moment might have been an unexploded bomb. (If you were to find one anywhere I guess this would be the place – the Cape is rich in military history and there are people up here who still swear the Japanese landed on our soil in WWII despite what the government would have us believe.)

That night the southeast wind rocking the bus put me to sleep, and when I woke it was blowing hard. I worked uninterrupted through the morning with only the wind for company, until sometime in the early afternoon a group of visitors came in, had a quick look at the ruins of the old landing, then left their mark at the message shelter and drove out.

Ten minutes later I heard a cheery, "Hello, is anybody in there?" coming from outside my bus.

It was a young woman of a likely age standing under my awning wanting to know how the fishing was, and given the short space of time between my only visitors leaving and her appearance I thought she must have been travelling with them. But no, she was doing a solo 4x4 trip around the country trying to find herself and hallelujah, she found me instead; probably not quite what she had in her mind's eye when she set off but if she was disappointed she didn't show it, and I had a pot of tea made before she had a chance to escape.

So we chatted and exchanged abridged life histories as single people do to test the waters, and such was the warm and friendly nature of our conversation I made a second pot of tea, and was just on the verge of thanking the universe for this lovely gift on such a wild and woolly afternoon, when she stood and thanked me for the tea and left. Just like that.

Well, to say I was disappointed is to say Hitler was a naughty boy. I had already decided on the meal I would cook for her and imagined how the wind would catch the secrets we whispered to one another before carrying them up into the starry sky. Okay, that's a bit rich, but I *was* hungry and starting to think about food and the wind *was* still blowing. And to be honest I *was* thinking how nice it would be to have company on such a night.

But I've snatched defeat from the jaws of victory many times before, and Captain Billy Landing isn't what you'd call a *recognised* pickup spot, I consoled myself as I cooked and ate a lonely meal of pasta with chorizo, Spanish onion and capsicum in a rich tomato sauce with freshly grated parmesan for garnish. And at this point I know I should say the food tasted of failure and I couldn't eat more than half, but it was really very good and I scoffed the lot with nary a backward thought. Indeed it was so good I decided to eat the second helping I tend to dish up when I make pasta, and I'd just set it before me when there she was, driving her 4x4 right back into my life as if she'd never left.

"Hi," she said.

"Hi," said I.

"There was a tree."

"A tree?"

"On the track"

"Oh, I see, a tree. Lucky me."

Shakespeare never knew such eloquence as she climbed from her car showing me the proof on her digital camera and me protesting that her word was good enough for me I didn't need to see the tree and I certainly wasn't accusing her of felling the tree just to have an excuse to come back and see me but she insisted there look at the size of that thing I couldn't move it on my own no of course not you were right to come back and here you are.

"Yes, here I am."

"Would you like some dinner? I've just eaten, actually," and I followed her gaze to the bowl of pasta before me, then to my raised fork, then back to the bowl.

"Really?" She looked doubtful.

"Oh, this? No this is just a spare I had lying around. I was about to make a pig of myself. I already ate mine, really. Wasn't expecting company, you know. I know it's only early but I like to eat before the sun goes down. Sometimes I even get to bed before dark. Not that I'm suggesting anything, of course. Don't be thinking I…"

"Shh," she said, mercifully. "Yes, I'd love something to eat, thank you."

So I relaxed and she ate and we picked up where we left off that afternoon, and we walked the beach into the sunset just like they do in the better movies, and bared our skin to the wind just like they do in the other movies, and the night was a tiny island in the lee of the storm and the morning came fine and clear.

"Right, I suppose we should get that tree cleared for you so you can get out."

"I suppose we should."

So I gathered my axe and bushman's saw and we drove in her car to the fallen tree. It was indeed a serious piece of rainforest hardwood and three or four swings of the axe told me it wasn't going to be dismembered that way, at least not in my lifetime. So we set to work pulling the tree apart limb by limb, using a chain attached to her winch to rip and snig the branches clear of the main trunk, before paring it back to a manageable size her little 4x4 could tow to the side of the track. We made a good team, but it was hot, hard work climbing and shackling and manoeuvering the limbs out of the way and the water she gave me tasted sweet at the finish. She watched me drink my fill and then smiled warm and cheeky.

"Ah, the lengths you men will go to in order to get rid of a woman," she said.

"Well at least I didn't have to chew off an arm," I said, and the rainforest swallowed our laughter.

Like I said, sometimes you just get lucky.

POINT OF THE MATTER

Then I walked to the northernmost point of the mainland again, over the rocky headland and through the blustery wind, to have my picture taken – read self-videotaped – beside the sign at the tip like so many other Australians have done before, and reflected on the changes since my last visit.

The last time I came was on the ill-fated Range Rover expedition for the Today Show in the early 1990s when we returned one vehicle short. This time I looked for the spot where my cameraman rolled his vehicle on the drive out and couldn't find it. The road was narrower than I remember and the scrub looked thicker, like it had grown over my past.

The Pajinka Wilderness Lodge at the very tip, too, was unrecognisable. I remember sitting around the rainforest bar having beers with the crew and thinking what a great resort location it was, what a great country. But this time all that remained was a scattering of vandalized and graffiti-covered ruins now being consumed by the jungle. There's been much gossip and innuendo regarding its demise and everyone has their own truth, but what we are fairly sure of is there was a disputation over the lease terms and shortly thereafter a fire destroyed some infrastructure and vehicles and it never re-opened for the 2002 tourist season. Looting and the natural order of the rainforest seem to have done the rest.

Even the old "You are now standing on the northernmost point of mainland Australia" sign at the tip was missing, presumably souvenired by some high-spirited tourist. In its place was a number plate with the hand-painted words "Most northern point Australia" donated by the Griffiths of NSW, who also added the warning, "Do not steal – we are watching."

I know the purists see this is as a terrible act of vandalism and I'm told it even made the news when the theft was discovered, but it's just a sign, after all. And there's something very Australian about knocking off an icon like the tip sign. Just as there's something equally Aussie about the Griffiths family supplying a substitute, complete with warning. Perhaps it's my iconoclastic nature but I also appreciate the witty additions to the road signs along the way. Cape York is "Dip" country and there's some very droll work on display, such as the old chestnut "Dip *me in honey and feed me to the lesbians*" and "*Skinny* Dip" and my personal, sick favourite "Dip *theria*".

One thing that hadn't changed was the road. It was a bastard then and it certainly hadn't improved; in fact if anything it was worse. It's only about thirty or so kilometers from Bamaga to the tip but the corrugations were hand made in hell. You can negotiate the dips and bumps, you can deal with the creek crossings and the odd fallen tree, but the constant jarring from the corrugations will shake the bones from your body and the life from your car.

Naturally, Claude took this as his cue to stop. Both front shockies gave out, and since I wasn't driving back down the Cape road without shock absorption and I couldn't get any replacements from Japan in short time I found myself stranded in the NPA (which doesn't refer to the northernmost point of Australia but the Northern Peninsula Area).

The NPA consists primarily of five communities: Bamaga, the main centre founded in the 1940s by settlers from Saibai Island in Torres Strait (Australia's first climate change refugees?); Seisia, the other Islander community providing a port service and arguably the most tourist-oriented facilities in the area; New Mapoon, the Aboriginal community established to house people relocated against their will from Old Mapoon, north of Weipa, when bauxite was discovered on the western Cape; and the two other Aboriginal communities to the south of Bamaga, namely Umagico and Injinoo, both well-situated on the sandy foreshores of the northern Gulf of Carpentaria. It's an interesting mix in a beautiful setting and quite unlike anywhere else in the country. At another time I could easily imagine burrowing in and learning more.

But I had other matters to attend. I had to find a way to get Claude the Belligerent and my tired self home. Suddenly I'd run out of steam. Six months of single-handedly sourcing, shooting, editing and writing stories, all the while battling technology and nursing and cajoling Claude along had done me in. Maybe it happened when the decision was taken out my hands, like a virus will hit you when you relax after a long period of stress. I was planning to return via the west coast and include Weipa and maybe some Mitchell River country in the Tourism travelogue. And I'd certainly promised the people at Moreton Telegraph Station that I'd return to shoot some more video of their resident Palm Cockatoos. But even the best-laid plans don't always hatch.

After a couple of days of exhausting my options with the regions' mechanical fraternity I realized I was going to need a 'get out of jail' card from a higher entity. It came to me while I was fishing.

Like all good wharfs the one at Seisia provides a wonderful community service, especially when the mackerel and trevally are running. The locals arrive in numbers to catch the baitfish that balls up in a black mass between the pylons, before hooking and casting the silvery slivers into the deeper water where the predators lurk. It's a lively scene with families and dogs and flapping fish all over the joint, and somewhere between the orange of the setting sun and the promise of the turquoise sea hangs the colour of expectation, for you never quite know what you're going to catch off the Seisia wharf. And it was while filming a giant cod hoovering a whole trevally from someone else's line – not mine, thankfully – that it occurred to me I could catch a ship from this wharf, a big ship, back to somewhere the roads would be kinder on a tired old bus driver and his temperamental charge.

I'd seen the Sea Swift ship come and go when I first arrived – indeed I'd even videotaped it for generic purposes – and after a few enquiries I learned the passenger vessel, the Trinity Bay, left weekly for Cairns, although it was usually heavily booked through the dry season. But a heartfelt email pitch to their marketing man and promise of inclusion in the Tourism travelogue as a wet season option for late travellers, secured berths for Claude and me for the following Monday. Hallelujah! That Claude would have to suffer the indignity of being manhandled by a forklift and spend the trip below deck, while I enjoyed the sights and the delights of the Trinity Bay as she skirted the coast back to Cairns was of no concern to me: he deserved it. My only concern was finding somewhere pleasant to hole up for the rest of the week while I waited for my ship to come in.

By pure co-incidence it happened to be Bamaga's busiest time of the year leading up to and including the Dan Ropeyarn Memorial weekend, when nine regional teams and their supporters came from all over the Cape, the NPA and Torres Strait to enjoy the knockout rugby league carnival. Again, at another time I might have got involved (for the record the Regional Pacific Argan Warriors beat the Injinoo Crocs in an extra-time nail-biter). But I wanted peace, and one of the locals directed me to Umagico Beach where I found an out-of-the-way caravan park in a setting as beautiful as its name. The facilities were basic and the ants were ferocious, but for me it was perfect.

So the last days of the trip were spent catching up on some editing, drafting a chapter or two and gazing out over the tropical water to the islands dotted in the Strait; islands I was told could be hopped by dinghy all the way to Papua New Guinea. The prospect intrigued me.

Customs and Border Protection currently operates less than a dozen pursuit vessels between Cairns and Broome, a fetch of several thousand kilometres of coastline taking the most direct route. Combined with aerial and local surveillance and military intelligence this, for now at least, appears to be doing the job of protecting our northern border. But what happens when low-lying Southeast Asia goes under water and the trickle of refugees becomes a deluge? Whatever your stance on global warming there is already clear evidence that many islands in Torres Strait are being inundated by rising sea levels (Saibai was merely the first), so it's reasonable to assume there's worse to come. Do we really expect to protect our privileged Australian way of life from the desperate needs of our neighbors with a handful of patrol boats and a squadron of Dash 8s with "Bugger Off" painted on their wings?

And which privileged Australian way of life are we protecting anyway? Is it the fast-disappearing one of the pioneers and schemers and dreamers, of the wanderers and misfits and stubborn believers the like of which gives heart to these books* and always gave this country a certain idiosyncratic charm and, dare I say, *Australian-ness*? Or are we protecting an urbanized, homogenized way of life no different to any other in the western world, where we make Faustian deals just so we can die with a few more toys and our children are so indulged they consider not upgrading to the latest Ipod the ultimate personal sacrifice, where conservatism is the new left and political correctness the new right, and all the while the disenfranchised eat a little more dirt and the rich put a little more distance between them and the pack and the seeds of racial hatred slip through the cracks of a tainted past and germinate on our bloodied streets?

I fear it is the latter, and while I'm aware these are no more than the futile ramblings of someone who spends too much time alone with his thoughts, I do worry about such things, as I'm sure others do. Just as I'm sure others worry about what sort of country we'll be leaving to our children, what sort of world. But I have no clever solutions to offer, and I know the whole catastrophe will play out as it must, as it always did.

But I'd still like to stand at the tip once more before I die, to feel the wind in my face and laugh at the bodgy sign provided courtesy of Jones or Jabanardi or Jamil El-Haq I don't mind, and be thankful I was born in a country that still has space, and life, and therefore, we must believe, hope. And maybe, after all, that's the best I can do.

* The **RED IN THE CENTRE** series.

ABOUT THE AUTHOR

Monte Dwyer is best known in Australia as the Today Show's slightly unhinged weatherman, a role he filled for over a hundred years. These days he's a professional vagrant, travelling the land in a badly behaved bus called Claude, collecting stories from the Australian bush for telling in his books and DVDs. He is also a vocally challenged singer/songwriter with recording credits too questionable to answer. In a land 'of beauty rich and rare' he is uncommonly common, poor and happy.